IGNORANCE IS NOT BLISS

A Primer for Authors—Protect Your Work and Yourself

Patricia Reding

Paperback
ISBN-13: 978-0-9982767-6-2
ISBN-10: 0-9982767-6-6

EPUB:
ISBN-13: 978-0-9982767-7-9
ISBN-10: 0-9982767-7-4

Website: www.PatriciaReding.com

Formatting: Polgarus Studios at www.PolgarusStudio.com

Cover: Cover Designs by James, at www.GoOnWrite.com

Scripta Manent Publishing
WRITTEN WORDS REMAIN

DEDICATION

This handbook is dedicated to all authors (and particularly to U.S. based authors) who seek basic information about how to protect their intellectual property rights—and how to avoid infringing on the rights of others.

Contents

AN INTRODUCTION AND A CAUTION

Hello, readers!

I would like to take a minute to introduce myself. As my fiction author profile mentions, I am an attorney by day and an author by night. I've practiced in the area of "intellectual property" law for . . . well . . . for decades. Intellectual property—valuable property that you cannot "touch" includes such things as trademarks (brands) and copyrights.

When I first started publishing my own fiction works and was introduced to authors around the country (and indeed, around the world), I quickly became aware of how little many of my fellow authors know about important legal issues that are of concern to them—whether they are aware of the issues, or not.

I think authors should: (1) have a general understanding of what to do if someone infringes on their intellectual property rights; and (2) have a general understanding about what they might do to avoid infringing on the intellectual property rights of others.

This handbook is not intended to be a definitive treatise on the issues presented. Rather, it is a primer, intended to provide you with general information about the issues so that you are prepared to ask the right questions. The answers to those questions will help you to protect your legal rights and they will help to keep you from finding yourself on the wrong end of an infringement claim.

As noted, I am an attorney. But I am not *your* attorney. Accordingly, the information provided herein, is for general education purposes only. The particulars are based on U.S. law at the time of publication. It is not intended to serve as, nor should you take it as, legal advice offered to you or to anyone else.

Chapter 1
An Overview

If I had a nickel for every time I heard an author suggest that he is flattered when a party illegally posts his work on a site and then allows others to freely download copies (to pirate the work), I would drop this project right here and right now—and I would retire . . . in luxury. I could afford to, after all. It is nothing short of astounding to hear someone say that they so want readers, that they will allow others to steal their good works. I suppose it's because for many, the art of writing is just that: art. Those creative souls who seek to change the world one reader at a time are not generally so interested in determining steps they should take to protect themselves. Still, the serious artist owes it to herself to find out how to do just that—and I suggest she do so quickly. In the process, she'll also learn something about how to avoid creating legal problems for herself with respect to using the works or portions of the works of others.

The area of the law that most authors know nothing about—but that they would be wise have at the top of their list for things to learn about—is "intellectual property." Uh-oh. There I've done it. I've used a legal phrase that I'm sure will have some folks rolling their eyes, and others about to give up—before they've even begun. But you should have no fear. The concept is simple, really. Something that is deemed to be "intellectual property" is, essentially, something of value that you cannot touch. Add in a general discussion about some contracts terms (which really relate for the most part with what may be done with an author's intellectual property), and some basic facts about ISBN numbers (because they may be helpful and may affect what, where, and how you can publish your works) . . . and you have an excellent list of the legal things about which an author most needs to know.

TYPES OF INTELLECTUAL PROPERTY

At the outset, I want to make something abundantly clear. Fairly frequently people will say (I practice in this area, so I hear these things regularly) that they want to protect their "idea." Well, I've little more to say about that, than this: "Good luck." Why? Because the *general* principle is that you cannot protect an *idea*. Once it is set out into the marketplace, it is available for the taking and using. There are, however, "exceptions." Ahhh . . . now we are getting serious.

The exceptions that allow one to protect an *idea* relate essentially, to whether it is: (1) patentable; (2) a trade secret; (3) trademark protectable; or (4) if it is set out in a "form" that is copyright protectable.

You'll be pleased to learn, I'm sure, that for the most part, only two of these will matter to authors. But first—an overview . . .

Patents

Essentially something is patentable if it is a new or useful process, machine, composition of matter, or an improvement of one of those things. Once all the requirements are met, and after the inventor applies for protection, the law may grant a patent. A patent gives the owner a period of time during which he and no other—without his "permission" or "license"—can make that same product, or use that same process, etc. Patents are issued for things like inventions of new machines (think a new type of toaster), the look of a particular product (think the design of an APPLE® iMac®); or a new variety of a plant (think a new hybrid tea rose). You will typically find something that is patented, identified by the symbol: ℗

I can hear you already. Likely, you're thinking: "But I'm a writer. I don't do that." You are correct—you are, and you don't. So it is highly unlikely you'll ever need to concern yourself with patent rights. On the upside, you won't misuse the word "patent" to identify other types of intellectual property in the future—and that is a bonus, since now you'll come across as the most well-versed amongst those in your writing group the next time you meet.

On we go then, to item two.

Trade Secrets

Another type of intellectual property asset is a "trade secret." A trade secret can be any type of information that cannot be readily determined by looking at a product and/or by reverse-engineering it. It may have to do with the way it is built, or it could include something like a secret ingredient or formula (such as, for example, the recipe for Coca-Cola®). The thing about trade secrets is that they are only protected for so long as they are kept "secret." The owner is required to take appropriate action to protect the secret if it is to remain one. As soon as the owner publishes the information, or fails to adequately protect it as a trade secret, or someone figures out the process or the ingredients (for example)—and assuming the party did not do so illegally (such as by putting a spy into the ranks of their competitor's employees)—it is no longer a protectable trade secret. Thus, the "idea" is out in the marketplace for use by others.

What does that have to do with authors? Not much—except that if you present your ideas to particular parties, such as publishers or movie producers, they may be required by law, or by a contract you enter into with them prior to your disclosure of the information to them, or both, to keep the information confidential. Beyond that? Very little—unless you have a secret formula for creating great works. If that's the case: mum's the word. Shhhh. Don't tell anyone.

Trademarks - Service Marks - Brands

The next category of intellectual property is one that every author needs to know something about. That is the area of trademarks, or brands.

Quite simply, a trademark is any symbol, word, slogan or tagline, logo, sign, mark, stamp, badge, color, sound, or smell, that identifies or represents a particular origin for some goods and/or services. We typically call a mark that is used for goods, a "trademark," and one that us used in connection with services, a "service mark." Sometimes people call these "brands."

The party using a trademark may identify the mark with the use of a symbol, as follows:

- Use the ® symbol for federally *registered* trademarks.
- Use the ™ symbol for unregistered trademarks. You may also use this symbol for registered marks, but there's no sense doing so when you can use the registration symbol.
- Use the ℠ symbol for unregistered service marks. Again, you may use this symbol for registered service marks as well, but there is no reason to do that if the mark is registered.

As noted, a party is not to use the ® symbol with a mark unless it is federally registered. On the other hand, the ™ and the ℠ symbols are used to indicate to others that the user of the mark claims trademark (or service mark) rights in the mark, although that party may not have registered the mark.

For the ease of reference going forward, I will refer to all trademarks and service marks simply as "marks" or as "trademarks." Also, I will refer to the goods or services that may be offered with those marks, as "goods/services." Finally, while I may identify a trademark owner's business name in regular typestyle (Apple Inc.), I will identify specific word marks in all capital letters (APPLE® Computers).

Authors should know something about trademarks—because they use them. Examples *might* include titles to products (discussed more fully, later), an author's own name (also discussed more fully, later), and/or the publisher's imprint that an author might use (if he is self-published and he uses a publisher's imprint). It is also helpful for authors to know when their works encompass the trademarks of others, so that they use them correctly. (Note: A publisher's imprint is merely the publisher's name under which works are published.)

Copyright

Copyright is a form of protection that the law grants to a party that is the creator of "an original work of authorship fixed in a tangible medium of expression." In other words, it is an original "idea," if you will, that a party puts into writing, or that he records, or paints, or sculpts, for example. Copyright protects the *form* that idea takes, not the *idea* itself. For example, I could not publish a story elaborating upon or revising portions from a Harry Potter tale without infringing on the copyright to those works. I could, however, write a story about an orphan boy wizard who attends a special academy and who is befriended by the schoolmaster.

A copyrighted work may be identified with the © symbol. The symbol ℗ is also used to provide a copyright notice for sound recordings (having originated from the use of the letter "P" for "phonogram").

Licensing Rights and Assignments

The owner of intellectual property, including trademarks and copyrights, may license his rights to others. If you think about it, the rights that are granted under a license constitute something valuable that you cannot see or touch. Likewise, an owner may assign to another, his entire interest in some of his intellectual property.

An author would be well advised to know about what to do to license her rights to others. An author also needs to know what to do when she needs to get a license to use the work or some portion of the work of another.

WHO IS LOOKING OUT FOR YOU?

Literary Agents

If you are represented by a literary agent, keep in mind that his duty is to get your work to a publisher—not to look out for your every legal interest. Thus, your agent's first concern will not be about intellectual property rights that you may wish to retain or to exploit (use) in some particular fashion. Rather, her primary interest is to get you "to a contract" and to get your work published and selling. So before you sign anything—including an agreement with a literary agent—please seek legal counsel.

Legal Counsel

When you hire legal counsel, her duty is to *you.* She will help to ensure that what you are signing, and that the rights you may be dispossessing yourself of, meet with *your* long-term plans and goals.

Of course, it goes without saying that although I am an attorney—I am not *your* attorney. Accordingly, I am not giving you legal advice through this work, merely providing you with general information.

Chapter 2
A Closer Look at Trademarks

Let's take a closer look at trademarks.

As previously mentioned, a trademark is any symbol, word, slogan or tagline, logo, sign, mark, stamp, badge, color, sound, or smell, that represents a particular origin (or source) for the goods/services offered with the mark.

SYMBOLS

As to symbols, consider the following:

Do you recognize the above? If you are a LV aficionado (as I admit, am I!), you do. You know that these marks represent a party that offers high price-point luxury luggage, handbags, and various additional elite consumer goods. The above are all trademarks, as are some of the individual component parts of some of the above. That is, the LV symbol, and the "words" LOUIS VUITTON—whether stylized in the specific manner shown above or in any other typestyle—are also trademarks.

How about this one? Do you recognize it?

Yes, that's right. It's the symbol for MERCEDES BENZ. When you see this on a car, or used in connection with car parts or car repair shops, you know that the vehicle is a Mercedes and/or that the parts are either provided by Mercedes or by someone else authorized by Mercedes for use with a Mercedes vehicle, and/or that the services are either provided by Mercedes, or by "affiliates" authorized by Mercedes to repair their automobiles.

Notwithstanding the above statements, it is possible for parties not explicitly "authorized" by Mercedes to make use of the word mark, MERCEDES BENZ for certain purposes. That is, a party may state that he repairs MERCEDES BENZ vehicles, although he could not use MERCEDES BENZ to identify his business (such as in "Joe's MERCEDES BENZ Repair Shop").

A party also may use the MERCEDES BENZ mark when referring to the product itself. Thus, a car parts provider that is not related to Mercedes Benz, could say that a particular part would fit a specific MERCEDES BENZ vehicle, although he should not use more of the mark than necessary to do so. Thus, he may be able to say on the packaging for a part: "This part fits a 2017 Mercedes Benz SLC Roadster." However, he could not use the mark in a manner that could confuse consumers. Thus, he should not use the symbol/logo shown above on the packaging, as it could confuse consumers such that they would believe that the product was an authentic MERCEDES BENZ part (that it was manufactured by that party), or that it was made by a Mercedes Benz authorized car parts manufacturer. Likewise, an unauthorized party should not say: "A *genuine* Mercedes Benz® part" to identify his product.

WORD MARKS

"Word" marks are words that are used to identify an origin of specific goods or services. So again, the words LOUIS VUITTON, like the words MERCEDES BENZ—(and in this case also their acronyms and/or abbreviations, namely, LV and MERCEDES), are considered "word" marks. So, too, are the following:

- APPLE
- HP
- EXXON
- VERIZON

When consumers hear or see these marks, they identify them as used in connection with specific goods/services.

TAGLINES OR PHRASES

Do you recognize any of the following?:

- WHAT'S IN YOUR WALLET? (CapitalOne)
- WHAT HAPPENS HERE STAYS HERE (the City of Las Vegas)
- WHAT CAN BROWN DO FOR YOU? (UPS)
- MELTS IN YOUR MOUTH, NOT IN YOUR HAND (M&Ms);
- CAN YOU HEAR ME NOW? (Verizon)
- WHEN IT ABSOLUTELY, POSITIVELY, HAS TO BE THERE OVERNIGHT (FedEx)
- WHERE'S THE BEEF? (Wendy's)

These are all slogans and/or taglines that were at the center of massive marketing campaigns. Consumers readily recognize them as identifying the origin of specific goods or services. These taglines serve as trademarks. When consumers see them, they recognize the parties with which they are associated.

SOME "ODD" MARKS—COLOR, SOUND, AND SMELL

So what's this about color acting as a trademark? Well, what color do you associate with Home Depot? Yes, that's right: orange. How about Target stores? Right again: red. Boxes from Tiffany's? Correct again: blue. Color makes up an odd category of trademarks.

Another unusual category of marks is "sound." For example, Harley-Davidson owns a sound trademark in the form of its unique engine sound. Another example is 20th Century Fox's "fanfare" at the opening of its movies.

Finally, "smell" can operate as a trademark. Specifically, one may use a unique scent to identify specific goods or services. Examples include the use of a flowery-musk scent in Verizon stores; a bubble gum scent for sandals; and a strawberry scent for toothbrushes.

But you are right, of course. As an author, you almost certainly don't care about these odd marks—unless you intend to have all of your books printed in a particular shade of chartreuse, open all your audio books with a unique sound or recording, and/or have all your goods manufactured with a predetermined scent that you want to protect . . . (For more on the manner in which color may play a part with trademarks, however, take note of my discussion of the FOR DUMMIES book series mark in Chapters 3 and 6). In any case, whether or not color, sound, and/or smell marks are of particular interest to you, from here on you'll at least be able to identify them properly for what they are.

FAMOUS MARKS

Once in awhile, a mark is so well known by the general consuming U.S. public, that it is deemed to be "famous." This really means that the mark enjoys a very broad zone of protection. With a famous mark, the owner may be able to stop others from using marks that would lessen the mark's uniqueness, even when they are not used on the same types of goods/services or with related goods/services. Examples of famous marks may include APPLE, DISNEY, and COCA-COLA.

Chapter 3
Trademarks of Specific Interest to Authors

Marks come in two types: those that are "registrable," and those that are not registrable and/or that are only used as "common law" marks.

WHAT IS AND IS NOT A REGISTRABLE MARK?

The U.S. Patent and Trademark Office (the USPTO), has a Trademark Register. Marks that meet certain criteria may be registered with the USPTO. Sometimes a mark may be used, and the user may have value in the mark, but it is not registrable, or the user may simply choose not to register it. This is acceptable in the U.S., where we say that the first party to "use" a mark is the owner of the mark. In other words, a party does not have to register a mark in the U.S. in order to claim ownership rights in and to the mark in the U.S. We call unregistered marks, "common law" marks.

Each of the 50 states also has a trademark register. I'll comment more on state registers, later.

Titles

Not infrequently, authors ask if they can trademark the titles to their works. The easy answer is: no . . . but . . . *maybe.*

The basic rule is that one cannot register the title *to a single work* as a trademark. This is because the law treats all single-work titles as though they did nothing more than "merely describe" their contents. Why does that matter? Because you cannot claim exclusive rights to the use of words or phrases that others may need to use so as to describe *their* goods. So even if a single title is widely promoted and has met with great success, if it is not used as something more than just as a title, it is not capable of trademark registration without something more.

Notwithstanding the general rule, you can register as a trademark, a series title. Examples of series titles include: FOR DUMMIES; CHICKEN SOUP; and NANCY DREW. The idea is that with a series title, consumers can expect, and that they have come to expect, that new works under that same series title, also come from the same source.

The Look of Your Product - Trade Dress

You may find ways to claim trademark rights with respect to the "look" of your products (your books), expressed in such ways as the cover copy design/format. Again, think of the FOR DUMMIES books. They are all predominantly in yellow, with a wide black band in which the title is placed, which in each case also includes the phrase FOR DUMMIES in a particular font—also in yellow. These features collectively (and some parts of them even individually) are trademarks that may be registrable.

Expanded Uses

As you expand what you do with your titles—that is, as you offer subscription newsletters, speaking services, and so forth, in connection with a "title," you may have trademark rights in that mark for those additional goods/services.

Indie-authors are always looking for new ways to sell their books, as well as for new ways to expand their income generating abilities. They may do this through the sale of related goods and services. When an author uses a title for these added goods and services, the author builds value in that "title" as a trademark. Consequently, he won't want others to take advantage of that value—to try to "pass off" their goods/services as though they came from the same source.

Names as Trademarks

In general, a mark that consists primarily of a surname is not registrable. It may become so if the user can prove that it is not "primarily" merely a surname—that is, that consumers identify it as used for the purpose of identifying a specific origin of goods/services. For example, McDonald's Corporation may originally have had some issues in registering McDONALD'S for use with fast food restaurants. However, when consumers came to identify McDONALD'S not only as a *surname*, but also for its secondary meaning—as designating the origin of a particular type of fast food restaurant services—the mark became registrable. As a consequence of the use and registration of that mark, no other party with the surname McDonald's could use McDONALD'S as a mark in connection with the same or related goods/services for which McDonald's Corporation uses its mark.

Names of Authors/Artists

The USPTO provides that any mark consisting of the name of an author used on a written work or of an artist on a sound recording, must be *refused* registration *if* the sole purpose of the mark is to identify the writer or the artist. The author's/artist's name may, however, be registered if it is used on a series of works and if the application shows that the mark (that is, that the author's/artist's name) *identifies the source of the series* and not just the name of the author/artist. Thus, first, the name would have to be used on more than one work. Second, the party would have to be able to show that the name serves as a trademark—that it designates a specific origin of goods/services. The bar for the kind and amount of evidence required for this, is quite high.

Names of Living Individuals

In addition to the rules about the names of authors and artists, if any mark consists of the name of a living individual, the party the mark identifies must give permission for the registration of the mark. The reason for this is because the person whose name the mark represents, would be giving up some rights to the use of her own name for the future.

Consider, for example, what might happen if I granted my publisher the right to register my name as a trademark. (This discussion assumes that my publisher could provide the evidence necessary to prove that my name actually serves as a trademark—a source identifier.) If my publisher did in fact register my name, the rights to the use my name for the same or related goods/services in the future, would no longer belong to me. I would be precluded from using my own name for works I create in the future. This is the reason why, before the name of any living person may be registered as a trademark (assuming the other requirements could be met), the person whose name it is would have to give permission for that registration. A word of caution, then: think carefully about giving your permission for the registration of your name as a trademark for use in connection with books, book publishing, or other related goods/services that you may still want to offer with your name in the future.

An Example Illustration

Just for the fun of it, let's take a look at a mark of interest here. Specifically, the following mark is registered with the USPTO for use with the goods/services noted below:

Do you recognize this signature? It belongs to JK Rowling, author of the Harry Potter Series. This mark is registered for use with a wide variety of pre-recorded materials (audio goods, CDs, etc.); books and other printed materials (such as calendars and wrapping paper); clothing; games; providing online chat rooms; entertainment services (including an interactive website); and internet based social networking services. The mark consists of the author's name, in a particular stylized form. The owner is Joanne Rowling, a UK citizen. The registration includes the required statement that the name "identifies the nickname of JOANNE ROWLING, a living individual *whose consent is of record.*"

The reasons I use this as an example are two: (1) it is fairly uncommon to find an author's name registered as a trademark at all; and (2) the mark noted consists of the name, JK Rowling, in the specific stylized form presented. That means that the registration for this mark provides for protection of the name *in this stylized form*. Of course, since this mark is now on the U.S. Trademark Register, and given the unquestionable fame of it, I think it is safe to say that another party could not get a registration for the same name (J.K. Rowling), even in a uniquely different stylized form, for use in connection with goods/services that are the same as, related to, replacements for, or used in connection with, the goods/services covered in the JK ROWLING registration. Further, if another party tried to use the same name for such goods—even without trying to register it—I suspect they would find themselves in the midst of an enormous legal battle!

Hashtags

A hashtag consists of a word or phrase following the # symbol. Hashtags are often used on social media sites to identify a keyword or topic of interest.

Can a hashtag serve as a trademark? It is possible. However, for registration purposes, the USPTO would have to determine that the hashtag is used not only as a means of facilitating searches, but that it also serves as a source identifier—as something that identifies a particular source of goods or services. So, depending on how the hashtag is used, it could function as a trademark.

Remember that in general, a trademark is something you do *not* want others to use—except with your permission and/or to refer to you and/or your goods and services. By contrast, a hashtag is something that you *do* want to encourage others to use through various social media outlets. You could use a hashtag in connection with your work. However, policing the use of the hashtag by others so that they only use it to identify you and your work could prove highly difficult. Accordingly, hashtags do not generally make for good marks.

Domain Names

Like hashtags, domain names by themselves are not generally considered to be trademarks capable of registration. Rather, a domain name is deemed to provide an "Internet address," if you will. If, however, a domain name is also used as a source identifier, it may be registrable as a trademark.

Parody Marks

There may be times when one party tries to use a mark that is "like" the mark of another party in some way, as a parody. In trademark law, whether two marks may coexist or not depends on whether one party's mark is likely to cause confusion, to cause mistake, or to deceive consumers with regard to the mark of another.

Parody essentially consists of materials that imitate other materials, but the use is done for "comic" purposes, or even to ridicule another party. Party One may try to use a variation of Party Two's mark intending that the mark will cause consumers to *call to mind*, the mark owned by Party Two. However, Party One's use also intends to clearly make fun of Party Two. Thus, when the parody is strong, Party One might be able to use (and even to register) a parody mark. Basically, a true parody calls to mind Party Two's product while *also creating a distinction* between the two marks at issue because of the "joke" that Party One's mark conveys about Party Two.

Use of Famous Names in Titles - Unauthorized Biographies

A famous person can't stop someone from using his name in the title of/for an unauthorized biography *simply* on the grounds of trademark infringement. However, one does not enjoy the unrestrained freedom to use a famous person's name or likeness for general commercial purposes. For example, I might be able to publish an unauthorized biography of JK Rowling, but it is highly unlikely that I could publish *The JK Rowling Guide to Writing Great Fantasy* without encountering serious problems with JK Rowling.

Also bear in mind, when using the name of another—whether famous or not—that there are numerous laws about making false statements of fact about someone (which could give rise to defamation claims). (Incidentally, defamation consists of "libel," which is publishing a false statement about someone that is damaging to their reputation, *in writing*," and "slander," which is making a false *spoken* statement damaging to someone's reputation.)

In addition, the laws of the various states provide for some rights to "privacy" and for protections regarding the use of one's "likeness." This is important to remember when you look to use the image of someone on your book covers, for example. Thus, you might confirm that your cover creator has the appropriate model-release in place if the artwork includes the likeness of someone living.

Even the use of the likeness of a deceased person—in particular a deceased famous person—may present issues. Specifically, the estate of the individual may either want to stop your use, or seek compensation for it. In short, don't assume that the likeness of a person is available for your use simply because the person depicted, is deceased.

COMMON LAW TRADEMARKS

A party begins to accrue rights in a mark (in the U.S.), when the party begins to use the mark (in the U.S.). We call those rights "common law" rights. When you use your name—your brand—in connection with your works, you have some common law rights in it as a trademark, although those rights are likely to be narrowly construed.

WHY SHOULD YOU CARE ABOUT ANY OF THIS?

Authors should care about trademarks because their works are provided in connection with one or more marks or "brands." A trademark represents the "goodwill" that the owner creates through his exclusive use of a mark. For most authors, this begins with his or her name (although again, those rights are quite narrow). Some authors (particularly indie-published authors) may use additional trademarks. For example, they may use specific design features on all of their covers, one or more series titles, and/or one or more publishers' imprints (since the author would in that case also be the publisher).

Trademark infringement occurs when a party tries to use a mark that is the same as, or that is confusingly similar to, the rightful trademark owner's mark.

Chapter 4
Your Trademark Rights

It is helpful for authors to have an understanding about when they begin to accrue rights in/to a trademark.

GENERAL PRINCIPLES

In the U.S., a party begins to accrue rights in a mark when the party first uses the mark or when the party first files an application to register the mark with the USPTO indicating that he "intends to use" the mark in the future. (By contrast, in most other countries, the first party to *register* the mark is deemed to be the owner.)

A trademark owner in the U.S. does not have to register a trademark to have rights in it, but she may register it.

In the U.S., a party may not get a registration for a mark until she has actually used the mark with the goods/services that are identified in her application. In other words, you could not register a trademark for use with "books" as goods, or with "publishing books" as services, until you have actually used the mark on those books, and/or in connection with those services.

You could, however, file an "intent to use" application with the USPTO to seek registration of a mark for use with those goods/services before you actually use the mark on those goods/services.

PRIORITY AND "INTENT-TO-USE" APPLICATIONS

In some cases, the early filing of an intent-to-use trademark application can be of great importance. This is because the true and rightful owner of a mark in the U.S., is determined by which party has "priority" rights to the mark.

Generally, a party's "priority date" is the date he first used his mark. However, when someone files an "intent to use" application to register a mark that he has not yet used, his "priority date" is the date he filed his "intent-to-use" application.

As between two parties arguing over rights to a mark for use with particular good/services, the party with the earlier priority date "wins."

AN ILLUSTRATION

To illustrate the rules of priority, let's consider a scenario. If today, I started using the mark BEST PRACTICES FOR AUTHORS for a series of books (that is, I sold books in a series of books with that mark as of today), I could claim rights to the mark BEST PRACTICES FOR AUTHORS for use in connection with a series of books as of today's date. If I don't start using the mark today (that is, I don't actually provide goods/services with the mark as of today) but I intend to so do in the future, I could file an "intent to use" application with the USPTO to register the mark, today. In either case, my "priority date" would be today's date. If then, another party started using the same mark tomorrow in connection with the same, similar, or related goods/services, my rights would supersede that party's rights.

There are further complicated rules about such things as how broad a person's common law rights are, what happens when Party One seeks registration of a mark even though he already knows about Party Two's use of the mark, and so forth. (In short, Party One should not seek registration of a mark he knows Party Two to already have used. In fact, the application to register a mark with the USPTO includes a sworn statement that the applicant believes himself to be the true, rightful and *exclusive* owner and user of the mark. If Party One knows of a prior user of the same mark for the same goods/services before filing his application, it would be fraudulent for Party One to sign the application claiming to be the true, rightful and exclusive owner and user of the mark.)

THE LIFE OF A TRADEMARK

A trademark belongs to you for so long as you use it. The registration for a trademark belongs to the registrant for so long as he maintains the registration.

Chapter 5
Choosing a Trademark

When you are thinking of a title, consider whether you might in the future, use the title for a series and/or for expanded goods and/or services. With that in mind, not only do you want to avoid infringing on the mark of another, you also want to try to avoid using titles that are merely descriptive of what the reader will get. This is because other people will still need to be able to use the same words that you might consider using for the "plain meaning" that those words convey.

TYPES OF MARKS

We often say that words used to identify goods that may (or may not, as the case may be) serve as trademarks, fall into one of the following categories:

- Generic
- Descriptive
- Suggestive
- Arbitrary
- Fanciful

The above list is from weakest to strongest. The stronger the mark, the easier it is to register and to protect as against infringement by others in the future.

Generic

A word that is generic for the goods/services cannot be registered as a trademark for those goods/services. Thus, you may not sell apples (the fruit) and call them APPLES, intending to use that as a trademark, thereby foreclosing others from the ability to call their apples by the same generic term. The reason is because others who also offer the same goods (apples) must be able to use the term to identify their goods. You could, however, sell *computers* using the term APPLE. (More on that later . . .) You might also be able to use APPLES in a specific design/logo form, have common law rights in that design/logo form, and even get a registration for that design/logo mark. If you did seek registration for such a mark, you would have to "disclaim" exclusive rights to the use of the term APPLES when used in connection with apples, but you could still protect the design/logo form of the mark. The disclaimer would mean that you recognize that you could keep another party from using another design/logo mark that looks like yours in connection with the same, similar, or related goods, but that you also recognize that you could not keep others from using the same descriptive/generic word that your mark uses to describe their goods/services.

Descriptive

A mark is deemed to be "merely descriptive" if is conveys an immediate idea of an ingredient, quality, characteristic, feature, function, purpose, or use, of the goods/services in connection with which the mark is or will be used. The mark needn't be wholly descriptive, only descriptive of some aspect of the goods/services.

If a mark is deemed to be merely descriptive, at first glance, it might not be registrable. If, however, the user can show that it is not merely descriptive because it has gained "secondary meaning," it may be registrable. A mark has gained secondary meaning when the public has come to identify it as the source for specific goods or services. (You will recall that we discussed this same principal in connection with the use of the surname McDONALD'S for fast food restaurant services.)

We all come into contact with descriptive trademarks every day. For example, consider BEST BUY, or PAYLESS, to describe retail stores. These marks convey something about the services offered with them (retail stores featuring moderately priced electronic goods, and retail stores featuring low priced shoes, respectively).

One of the reasons descriptive marks are common is that marketing personnel typically seek to convey with a trademark, something about the goods or services offered with the mark. By contrast, we lawyers are forever trying to encourage our clients to choose things that are not descriptive. This is because non-descriptive marks are easier to register and to protect from infringement in the future. Consequently, a non-descriptive mark is a much more valuable asset in the long run.

Suggestive

A mark is suggestive when, as applied to the goods or services at issue, it may call to the consumer's mind, something about those goods or services. Basically, such a mark is one that requires some imagination to make the leap from the suggestion that the mark makes, to the goods/services offered with the mark. Examples of marks of this nature include such things as COPPERTONE for a tanning solution, or TINT TONE for hair coloring.

Arbitrary

An arbitrary mark is one that has a common meaning, but not as related to the goods/services offered with the mark. For example, APPLE is a common term, easily understood, spoken, and spelled. When used for selling apples (the fruit), it would be generic. But when used for computers, it is arbitrary.

Fanciful

A fanciful mark is one that is made up or invented solely for the purpose of functioning as a trademark. Examples of these marks include KODAK, EXXON and VERIZON. These are the strongest types of marks because they have no meaning outside of the use of them as trademarks.

A TEST CASE

What, you might ask, does this have to do with you and why should you care? Well, when you choose a title (that you may use for a series or in some other expanded ways, thereby opening up the possibility for registering it), or when you choose a publishers imprint, you are choosing a *trademark*.

To illustrate this, let's take a look at how I went about choosing my title for this work—a title I also use for additional services, such as for speaking engagements.

If I had tried to use something like the word, BOOK, for this handbook, clearly the title would have been generic. Thus, it would not be registrable (even if I used it for more than one book) or otherwise protectable. I could not stop others from calling one of their books a BOOK just because I used the generic term in connection with my products.

A proposed title like AN AUTHOR'S GUIDE TO HANDLING LEGAL ISSUES, or LEGAL CONSIDERATIONS FOR AUTHORS, would have been highly descriptive of this handbook and/or of other goods/services that I might offer with such a mark in the future. Eventually, I *might* be able to register such marks, but I'd never be able to stop others in the future, from using similar phrases as a part of their general use of the English language, to discuss the same general principles covered in their works as are covered in this work.

I actually chose something suggestive: IGNORANCE IS NOT BLISS, along with a subtitle. Essentially I took a common phrase, IGNORANCE IS BLISS, and revised it and added an (admittedly) descriptive subtitle to it, so as to convey the message I wanted to convey—that this work discusses legal issues that authors would be interested to know something about.

Note that I could have chosen something like NO BLISS, which would have been a fanciful mark, or even NOBLISS, which would have been an arbitrary mark in this context. Such marks would have made for strong marks for seminars and so forth, later. However, it is more difficult to build recognition in fanciful and arbitrary marks because they really don't even hint at the goods or services offered with them. (Having said that, if I did manage to build recognition in such a mark, I would have a stronger mark.)

I can use the title that I chose (in particular without the subtitle) to discuss a series of legal issues that author's face. I can also use it for speaking engagements, newsletters, webinars, and more. It is suggestive of what the consumer will get, but it is not merely descriptive of what the consumer will get. Thus, if a third party came along in the future and tried to use it, or something confusingly similar to it, in connection with similar goods/services, I could claim that that party's use infringes on my trademark rights.

THE STANDARD – CONFUSING SIMILARITY

A mark is available for use if it is not *likely to be confused* with a prior registered mark (or a mark that is pending registration)—or with a prior common law mark. Thus, whether or not you intend to register a mark, you should always consider whether it is likely to be confused with any prior registered marks or with any common law marks used by *other* parties. Preferably you will make this determination *before* you use your proposed mark. If you do not, another party could claim that you have infringed on her trademark rights.

Determining whether something is "confusingly similar," can be difficult. Essentially, one must decide if his chosen mark is likely to be confused with one or more prior registered, pending, and/or common law marks, after considering some common factors.

As words and phrases are in constant use, it is almost always the case that there is some risk associated with the adoption of any mark. Here is where I say that you must keep two basic principles in mind at all times:

- Reasonable people can differ.
- Not all people are reasonable.

Why do I say this? Well, as noted, there is almost always some risk with adopting a mark. So your goal before doing so, is to determine how high that risk is, and whether assuming that level of risk is acceptable to you. If you determine that the risks are "high" that your proposed mark is likely to be confused with another, you might choose something else before you actually use that mark. Having said that, even when you think the risks are low, you may be right, but remember—others may disagree. (That is, that not all people are reasonable.) In short, you cannot eliminate all risk. Still, you can reduce your potential risks. Keeping that in mind, try to choose marks that are as "clear" of potential risk as possible.

Before adopting a mark, you want to consider these three questions:

- Can I use it, or does another party's prior use of another mark, whether registered or not, preclude me from doing so because my mark would likely be confused with their mark, as a consequence of which they may bring an infringement action against me?
- Can I register it if I am so inclined, because my proposed mark is not generic and because there are no prior registered marks with which my proposed mark is likely to be confused?
- Can I enforce my rights in the mark in the future?

As to the last question, if after searching a mark, you determine that there are numerous users of highly similar marks for "related" goods or services that already coexist, we say that the protection that each of those prior marks enjoys, is narrow or limited. If you find that this is the case when you review a proposed mark, you may conclude that even a small change or differentiation between your mark and those prior marks is all that it would take to make your mark distinguishable from the others. In such case, you might reason that you may use your proposed mark—and maybe even that you could register it. Keep in mind, however, that going forward, you want as strong a mark as possible because you will want to be able to stop others from using things that are confusingly similar to your chosen mark.

In short, if you conclude that there are numerous users of similar marks such that if they can coexist, so too can your proposed mark, keep in mind that in such a case, it will be difficult to enforce your trademark rights in the future. By contrast, when you choose a strong mark, you enjoy a broader "zone of protection" for that strong mark. Thus, if in the future you find another party trying to use a similar mark with related goods/services, you could conceivably claim your superior rights to the mark, make the case that confusion between the two marks is likely, and even bring a trademark infringement action against that party.

Chapter 6
Trademark Searching

There are several ways you can proceed with searching a trademark. The best is to seek legal counsel and have him conduct a comprehensive search. Your attorney would take the information from that search and would identify for you, possible prior registered and pending marks that the USPTO might cite against your application to register your mark (if you tried to register it). Your counsel could also inform you of common law marks that may be of interest to you. He will then help you to assess the risks of adopting and using your proposed mark before you actually do so.

In practice, many people proceed without a comprehensive search, as such searches can be quite costly. While the approach is not recommended, if you intend to do this, then there are still a few things you can do in advance to help to protect yourself:

- Search the USPTO for prior registered and pending marks of interest
- Conduct online searching for common law marks of interest

- Particularly for titles you may use for additional goods and services, search sites where books and/or other similar or related goods/services are available, such as Amazon

We are going to take a look at a test case, but before we do, let's consider what it is that you would be looking for when searching a proposed mark to determine if it is available for your use and possible registration without a high risk of refusal by the USPTO, or of a third party's opposition to your use and registration of the mark.

THE "CONFUSING SIMILARITY" FACTORS

The most important factors to consider when determining whether confusion between two marks is likely (although there are additional factors that could be considered), include:

- How similar the marks are in appearance, sound, connotation and commercial impression
- How similar the goods or services offered in connection with the marks are (that is, whether they are the same as, similar to, used as replacements for, and/or are used in conjunction with, one another)
- How similar are the trade channels through which the goods or services will move (which may also tell us

something about how similar the consumers of those goods/services are likely to be)

- How sophisticated the consumers of the goods/services are
- The price of the goods/services and whether they are purchased though quick decisions or instead, only after careful consideration
- The fame of the prior registered mark
- How many other "similar" marks already coexist (that is, how "diluted" or, alternatively, how "strong" the prior registered mark or marks may be)
- Whether there has been any actual marketplace confusion to date (if you have already used your mark)
- The length of time that the marks might already have coexisted in the marketplace without confusion (again, if you have already used your mark)

APPLICATION TO A TEST CASE

With the above factors in mind, let's take a look at that test case.

When I considered my title for this work, which I now also use for related goods and/or services (such as speaking engagements), I took the above factors into consideration and played around with a few ideas.

An example of something I would *never* have considered trying to use, is THE LAW FOR (AUTHOR) DUMMIES. This is because the series title FOR DUMMIES is well known, and FOR DUMMIES is registered with the USPTO to John Wiley & Sons, Inc. ("JWSI").

If I tried to put out a book, or provide other goods or services with THE LAW FOR (AUTHOR) DUMMIES, JWSI would almost certainly demand that I cease and desist, and might even bring an infringement action against me, demanding that I disgorge any profits I earned on my sales. The same result could have occurred if I had tried to use something like THE LAW FOR THE UNINFORMED AUTHOR—and especially if I'd put it on a cover that was primarily yellow with a black band across it, in which the title appeared. In that case, JWSI might bring a claim based on the look (the trade dress) of JWSI's goods. JWSI would likely base its position on the following facts:

- My product would look similar to JWSI's own
- My product and title would have similar connotations to JWSI's mark and designs
- My mark would be used on the same types of goods as JWSI's goods
- My goods and JWSI's goods would pass through the same trade channels (which means that we both would be selling products on Amazon and/or in other book stores)
- My consumers and JWSI's would be the same, and they would not be "highly sophisticated" for purposes of the goods at issue (which just means that our consumers would be those looking for information about

something in particular, about which they know little or nothing—which by definition, both marks suggest)

- My goods and JWSI's goods would be priced low and purchases for them would be "quick" decisions (as opposed to the purchase for something like a car or a major appliance, for example, which would be made only after careful consideration)
- JWSI's mark, FOR DUMMIES, is well-known—as is the yellow/black cover color scheme for JWSI's products
- JWSI's mark, FOR DUMMIES, enjoys a wide zone of protection because it is the only mark that is registered and that is in use that encompasses the phrase FOR DUMMIES or something highly similar to it for use in connection with the same, similar, and/or related goods

In short, the question is not whether the marks at issue are *identical.* The issue is whether they may be confused by their similarities to one another.

Knowing all of this, FOR DUMMIES or FOR THE UNINFORMED AUTHOR were not title options I considered. Rather, I considered using IGNORANCE IS NOT BLISS.

Searching the USPTO

With my proposed trademark in mind, my first stop was the USPTO. At http://tmsearch.uspto.gov/bin/gate.exe?f=tess&state=4809:tgvn4l.1.1, are options for trademark searching.

You could begin with the "Basic Word Search Mark." Click on the link and in the next window that comes up, fill in the search term (or terms) of interest.

For my proposed mark, I searched IGNORANCE and BLISS together. The results showed three current "live" marks, one of which is/was identical to my proposed mark *in sight and sound.* The other two "live" marks really did not look and sound, overall, like my proposed mark, even though they both included the terms IGNORANCE and BLISS. I also took a quick look at the "dead" marks, because I know that someone's registration might have lapsed (because they failed to file something required to maintain that registration), but that the party might still be using the mark. Since the "dead" marks that came up in my search dated back some years, I essentially determined that it was not highly likely that the parties that had owned those registrations were still using those marks.

As noted, I found one "LIVE" prior registered identical mark, IGNORANCE IS NOT BLISS. It is registered for use with organizing and conducting volunteer programs and community service projects and conducting programs in the field of child development. My proposed title was not to be, and is not, used with goods/services that are the same as, or that are related to, those services. Further, my goods/services would pass through different channels to different consumers than those offered with that prior registered mark. Thus, I concluded that consumer confusion between that prior registered mark and my mark was not highly likely. Now it could be that the prior registered mark is so well known that its zone of protection expands beyond the services covered in the registration for the mark (that is, that it is a "famous" mark). However, I concluded that if the mark was that well known, I would have heard of it. As I had not, it didn't overly concern me.

Of course, I did not stop there. Do you remember that the test is "confusing similarity?" That's right. I'm not concerned only with *identical* marks. I also don't want my mark to be confused by its similarity to other marks. Thus, I then searched the USPTO for marks that shared IGNORANCE IS with my proposed mark. I found:

- PREJUDICE IS IGNORANCE, for children's clothing
- A mark that included the phrase IGNORANT SUPREMUS TYRANNOUS (which translated means IGNORANCE IS THE GREATEST TYRANT), used for promoting the interests of science and scientific research and for educational programs and workshops in the field of science
- IGNORANCE IS DEATH, used for clothing
- IGNORANCE IS NO DEFENSE, used for downloadable publications in the field of law, non-fiction books in the field of law, and providing legal information online

The last mark from this search, IGNORANCE IS NO DEFENSE, is used for things vaguely similar to those things I intended to provide with my mark. However, overall my mark appears sufficiently distinguishable from that mark in sight and sound, and my subject matter differs from what is covered with that mark, such that I concluded that consumers would not likely confuse the two marks. (Again, this discussion assumes that my title is or will be used in a manner that will allow it, ultimately, to be a registrable mark.)

Online Searching for Common Law (Unregistered) Marks

Next, I looked for common law marks of interest. For this, I went to GOOGLE, BING, and other search engines. First, I searched for uses of the identical "mark," IGNORANCE IS NOT BLISS.

I found a number of article titles similar to my proposed mark. However, I did not find the phrase used by another party as a trademark—to identify the source of goods or services. Of course, the number of records found in an Internet search is generally quite high. Thus, I only reviewed the first few pages of the search results. I anticipated that if someone was using IGNORANCE IS NOT BLISS as a trademark for books and/or speaking services, etc., that it would likely show up by then. (In other words, not knowing the information that digging further into the results might have revealed, was a risk that I will willing to assume.)

Next, I searched IGNORANCE BLISS BOOKS. With this search, I found references to a number of books with titles such as:

- IF IGNORANCE IS BLISS, WHY AREN'T THERE MORE HAPPY PEOPLE?, for a book on Amazon, under "humor"
- IGNORANCE IS BLISS, for a fantasy novel listed on inkshares.com
- IGNORANCE IS BLISS: A STORY PROVING THAT ONE MAN CAN MAKE A DIFFERENCE—UNFORTUNATELY, also for a book on Amazon under "humor" and "satire"
- THE BLISS OF IGNORANCE, for a book of poetry on Amazon
- IGNORANCE AND BLISS, for a dystopia novel mentioned on forwardreviews.com

I stopped there, determining that there were several additional uses of book titles that included the terms IGNORANCE and BLISS. Thus, I wanted to know if there were any other books that included IGNORANCE with NOT BLISS.

Searching these terms, I found:

- SWEET MELISSA: IGNORANCE IS NOT BLISS (Book One), for a book on Amazon under memoirs/women's fiction
- MISS INNOCENCE, OR, IGNORANCE, NOT BLISS, a novel by Alan Dale from 1891 at books.google.com
- IGNORANCE IS NOT BLISS: NEVER IGNORANT GAINING GRAMMAR

EDUCATIONAL REVOLUTIONARY, for a poetry book on Amazon

- IGNORANCE IS NOT BLISS: SEEK KNOWLEDGE FROM THE CRADLE TO THE GRAVE, for a book of poetry on books.google.com

Next, I went directly to Amazon.com and searched IGNORANCE IS BLISS and IGNORANCE IS NOT BLISS. There, I found a few of the books noted above, as well as the following:

- IGNORANCE IS BLISS . . . NOT!: JOIN THE EDUCATED, listed under law/taxation and business and money/taxation
- OUCH!: IGNORANCE IS BLISS, EXCEPT WHEN IT HURTS - WHAT YOU DON'T KNOW ABOUT MONEY AND WHY IT MATTERS (MORE THAN YOU THINK), about which no further information was provided, but which presumably, is about money and investments
- IGNORANCE IS BLISS: THE THINGS MEN DON'T KNOW AND DON'T WANT TO, listed under humor and entertainment
- WHERE IGNORANCE IS NOT BLISS, for a 1964 publication about which there was no further information
- IGNORANCE IN GOVERNMENT IS NOT BLISS, for a 1972 publication about which there was no further information

As I considered these titles, it was clear to me that they coexisted, apparently without confusion—and that none appear to be used as a series title. The first relates to money and taxation and may touch on the law. However, its focus is different from my own. Thus, it didn't overly concern me. Likewise, the other books noted covered topics unrelated to my own. Finally, in those few cases where no further information was available, the items dated back to the 1960s and 70s. It seemed to me that even if those works did cover legal issues—and in particular, those legal issues of interest to authors—that they would be long out of date.

Based on the above analysis, even if I did not conduct a "full" search (through legal counsel), I determined I could proceed with my proposed title. Does this mean that there is "no risk" that another party, and in particular the owner of the one identical registered mark that I found, will take action against me? No, it does not. Might someone, including the registered trademark owner noted above conclude differently than me? Yes, they might. Might that party be "unreasonable" to do so? In my estimation, yes, they would be. And so, I determined I would use IGNORANCE IS NOT BLISS.

In short, I found that with respect to my proposed title, there is/was some risk, but the risk seemed minimal to me and it seemed I would not be unreasonable to assume that risk.

APPLICATION TO ANOTHER TEST CASE

In addition to an author's name or a titles series name, it is not uncommon for authors, and in particular for indie-authors, to use a publisher's imprint. Mine is SCRIPTA MANENT PUBLISHING. I took SCRIPTA MANENT from an old Latin proverb, VERBA VOLANT, SCRIPTA MANENT, which literally translated, means SPOKEN WORDS FLY AWAY, WRITTEN WORDS REMAIN. To it, I added the tagline (the slogan) WRITTEN WORDS REMAIN. Thus, I claim trademark rights in SCRIPTA MANENT and in WRITTEN WORDS REMAIN, and in a "design" or "logo," form of this mark, for use in connection with books and book publishing, speaking services, and possibly for other goods and/or services that I may offer in connection with these marks in the future:

Before I adopted this mark, I searched the USPTO to confirm that there were no prior registered or pending identical or confusingly similar marks. In fact, I looked for any marks that shared the following combinations of terms:

- SCRIPTA and MANENT
- SCRIPTA and WRITTEN
- SCRIPTA and WORDS
- SCRIPTA and REMAIN
- MANENT and WRITTEN
- MANENT and WORDS
- MANENT and REMAIN
- WRITTEN and WORDS
- WRITTEN and REMAIN

Once I concluded that there were no prior registered or pending marks of particular concern to me, I also engaged in online searching to determine if there were other parties using something like my word mark—as a common law mark—for the same or related goods/services. Finding none, I reviewed books on Amazon and elsewhere. I did find some titles that shared SCRIPTA MANENT with my proposed mark. However, I found none of particular concern. Thus, I adopted the mark. I believe that it will be a strong mark going forward—and one that I could protect against infringement by others. (Might I be wrong? Yes, risks remain. However, those risks do not seem particularly "high.")

I'll note one last thing about my publisher's imprint. It includes design features. There are ways to search design features with the USPTO. (Searching common law uses of design features would be much more difficult since there is no readily available database for common law marks.) However, explaining how you would search a design mark goes beyond the scope of this work. If you are interested in such a search, your legal counsel could help you. In any case, once I reviewed the available information, I determined that I was willing to take the risk that another party does not use words in combination with design features that are so similar to my design mark, in connection with goods/services similar to my own, such that my mark was likely to be confused with any such uses. Accordingly, I adopted and now use, the mark.

A WORD ABOUT TRADEMARKS WITH DESIGN FEATURES AND COPYRIGHT

We will take a closer look at copyright issues later, but for now, simply note that the design features of a trademark may also be capable of *copyright* protection. (For more information, see Chapter 11.)

Chapter 7
U.S. Trademark Registrations

Once I have used a mark, I gain common law rights in and to the mark. Those common law rights essentially mean that I could stop (or at least try to stop) a third party from registering and/or from using, any other mark likely to be confused with my mark, when used in connection with goods/services that are the same or that are related to those I offer with my mark, and in the same geographical area in which I've used my mark. Since most authors' works are promoted via the Internet across the country, it is *possible* my common law rights would be deemed to be countrywide—even if at any given time, I'd only sold books into some smaller geographical areas within the U.S.

U.S. TRADEMARK REGISTRATION RIGHTS

If so inclined, I could seek a U.S. trademark registration for my mark. Registration would allow me a few added legal benefits. In particular, I would:

- Enjoy the legal presumption that I own my mark and the exclusive right to use it nationwide
- Have the right to use the ® symbol (sometimes called the "Circle R" or the "R-ball" symbol) with my mark
- Have the ability, in the event a third party infringed on my mark, to bring an infringement action against that party in a federal court

As to seeking registration with the USPTO, in some respects the process is not terribly complicated. However, it is easy for the layperson to get caught up with issues unknown to them. For that reason, if you want to register a mark, you would be wise to seek legal advice. You can help to keep your costs down by doing some preliminary searching before you contact her. Also, the more you understand of the registration process and what registration will provide to you, the less your counsel will need to explain to you. Again, this keeps costs down. (So, it's a good thing you're reading this now. Yes?)

APPLICATIONS FOR REGISTRATION WITH THE USPTO

For the sake of general information, I note that to apply to register your mark, you will need to know:

- The mark
- The owner's name, address and state of incorporation or residence

- The goods and/or services offered or to be offered with the mark
- If those goods/services have already been provided in U.S. interstate commerce, the date you first provided/sold those goods/services in commerce
- The name of the party who will sign the application for the owner (if the person is signing for a legal entity, such as for a corporation)
- The title of the party who will sign the application

In the U.S., a party may not get a registration for a mark until after the mark is actually used for the goods/services identified in the application for registration. However, a party may file an application to register the mark based on his "intent to use" the mark for the recited goods/services. In such case, the actual registration will not issue until the applicant can prove that he has used the mark with the goods/services recited in the application.

One reason the USPTO does not allow a party to get a registration for a mark before she has used the mark is that the USPTO does not want people buying and selling (trading in) trademarks willy-nilly and thereby filling the register with unused marks.

STATE TRADEMARK REGISTERS

Each of the 50 states and Puerto Rico also has its own trademark register. You certainly may file an application for a state registration. In truth, however, it wouldn't get you much.

Further, most books are sold online—nationally (if not internationally). Even so, individual state registrations are significantly easier to get than national registrations, they are less expensive than registrations with the USPTO, and a state registration may be better than nothing in terms of helping to put the world on notice that you claim rights in a mark.

The prior owner of a federal (USPTO) registered mark could still insist that you discontinue use of a mark that you've registered in one or more of the states, if that party registered his mark with the USPTO before you used and/or registered your mark in one of the states (and assuming that the party was also the first to use the mark if he didn't file an "intent-to-use" application to register the mark before you used your mark). In other words, he may still stop you if his priority date is earlier than your own. (For more on priority dates, see Chapter 4.)

There are complicated rules that apply when the junior-user (the second *user*) of a mark is the first party to gain a U.S. registration for the mark (that is, when he is also the senior *registrant*). Assuming that the junior user was not aware of another party's use before he got his U.S. registration, these rules will kick in. Essentially, we determine who has the greater rights to a mark by considering such things as what common law rights the senior user had before the junior user got his U.S. registration. In any case, in light of the complications of these issues, they are well beyond the scope of this handbook. If you encounter facts of this nature, by all means, see your legal counsel.

REGISTRATION ELSEWHERE

The above discussion is centered around the use and registration of trademarks in the U.S. In many other countries, the first party to *register* a mark is deemed to be the owner. (This is unlike the U.S. rule, which provides in general, that the first party to *use* a mark is deemed the owner—at least of some common law rights, although the extent of those rights is determined by the particular facts. The exception again, is that a party may gain rights to a mark by filing an application with the USPTO, indicating that party's "intent-to-use" the mark in the future.)

To complicate matters, in addition to the fact that different countries have their own trademark registers, there are also a couple of multi-country registers, such as the European Union Intellectual Property Office (EUIPO) Register. A registration with EUIPO provides the registrant with protection (currently) in over 20 countries.

For more information on international registrations, contact your legal counsel.

Chapter 8
Trademark Infringement

There are two times in particular, that you may need to know a little something about trademark infringement:

- When you believe that someone else is trying to trade on the goodwill you've created in your trademark (that is, that the party is infringing your mark)
- When another party contacts you, claiming that you are infringing on that party's mark

WHEN SOMEONE IS INFRINGING ON YOUR RIGHTS

A trademark owner possesses the exclusive rights to the use of his mark on or in connection with particular goods or services. If another party uses a mark that is confusingly similar to the owner's mark, he may—and perhaps even should—take action. (In fact, if he doesn't take action in a timely manner, he could eventually lose his ability to do so.)

Whether trademark infringement has occurred will depend

in part on who has priority rights to the mark.

Once again, the issue of priority is determined by considering when the respective parties first used the marks at issue; whether either party has any registrations for her mark; and whether either party filed an intent-to-use application to register her mark with the USPTO (assuming that the application eventually matured to registration).

The issues of what to do in the event of an infringement of your mark go beyond the scope of this handbook. If you discover what you think is an infringement of your mark, you should seek legal counsel in a timely manner. Chances are, he will begin the process by sending the other party a cease and desist letter. Having said that, there are times when an infringement is so egregious, and the likely harm to the rightful trademark owner so imminent and potentially permanent (and not capable of resolution through the simple payment of money damages—because the infringement also includes some sort of damage to the owner's reputation or to the reputation of his goods/services, for example), that other legal actions (such as filing in a court for an injunction that will order the other party to immediately discontinue use of the mark) may be in order.

Most trademark infringement matters do not go to litigation. Rather, most times, the parties work something out. For example, if you present another party with facts showing you are the rightful owner of a mark, the infringing party may simply agree to discontinue his use. Often he will do this after requesting a period during which he may divest himself of his remaining inventory. The rightful owner generally will grant that period, because the alternative costs of taking further legal action would be extremely time consuming and expensive.

WHEN SOMEONE CLAIMS YOU ARE INFRINGING ON THEIR RIGHTS

Imagine one day you get up and prepare to head to your office (or you sit down before your computer, dressed in your favorite footie jammies and with a coffee mug in hand) and the doorbell rings. You open it. The party at the door asks if you are who you are and then, as they hand an envelope over to you (and somehow you just know it is not to inform you that you are the next PUBLISHER'S CLEARINGHOUSE winner!), they say, "You have been served." Frantically, you tear the envelope open. Inside you find a summons and complaint, claiming you have infringed on the mark or marks of another party. You have days to respond.

Alternatively, suppose you get up to stretch your legs after hours of laboring on your current work-in-progress. You decide to go to get the mail. Inside the box is an envelope. Curious, as you note it's from a law firm, you tear it open, only to find a letter demanding that you immediately cease and desist in your use of one or more trademarks that another party claims belong to her.

What are you to do?

Well, first: don't panic. No, really, you shouldn't panic. Instead, contact your legal counsel as soon as possible. As discussed above, it is *likely*, although not a certainty, that you'll be able to work something out with the other party that will solve your legal issues short of a full-fledged lawsuit. After all, that party doesn't want the expense of litigation any more than you do.

As to the *practical* issues: be prepared. You may have to change your title(s), the cover(s) of your works (so as to change their appearance), or some other mark or marks you are using. Also, you may have to destroy inventory of your product that you have on hand. Such actions would be time consuming, difficult, and costly for you—but they would be nothing compared to the cost of defending yourself in a lawsuit. So, again, prepare yourself for changes that you might have to make—and be glad you are now better armed. With the information in this handbook, you are more likely to avoid possible future issues of a similar kind.

ASSIGNMENTS AND LICENSES

The owner of a USPTO registered mark has registration rights to use the mark for the goods/services identified in the registration *throughout the U.S.* If she has also used the mark on goods/services that are not covered in the registration, then she will also have common law rights to the use of the mark for those additional goods/services.

The owner of a registered mark may "assign" the registration rights that the party owns. So, if you own a registration for a title series trademark for use with books, but you also use that series title in connection with providing online information and materials regarding self-publishing, you could assign the registration of the mark for use with the goods (the books), as well as the common law rights you have to the mark insofar as you have used it in connection with providing online information and materials about publishing. Alternatively, you could assign the registration rights for use of the mark as a series title for books, and retain the common law rights to use the mark for other purposes.

In the U.S., if you want to assign a trademark registration to another party, the assignment must include all of the rights to the mark and the business associated with it, including the "goodwill" related to the mark for use with the particular goods/services at issue.

A mark owner may also license to other parties, rights to use his mark. In such instances, an agreement would be in order so as to provide where, when, and how, the other party may use the mark. Note that if you use/own a mark for a blog that provides specific types of information, you could license another party the right to use the mark for speaking engagements that offer the same type of information (provided, of course, that some other party does not already own rights to the mark for those purposes). If you license rights to use your mark to another party, you are obligated to make sure that the licensee provides goods/services that meet your standard of quality. You may not just license numerous parties to use the mark for various goods/services and then sit back to see what happens. Basically, if you do not do what is necessary to protect the quality of the goods/services offered with your licensed mark, you may be deemed to have "abandoned" your mark. And, of course, an abandoned mark is one that others may adopt and use without infringing on the rights of a prior owner.

Chapter 9
Copyright Basics

U.S. copyright law dates back nearly to the beginning of the country. In fact, the Constitution provides, at Article I, Section 8, Clause 8, that Congress shall have the power . . . "to promote the progress of science and useful arts, by securing for limited times to authors and inventors, the exclusive rights to their respective writings and discoveries." The theory behind the Constitution and the laws that put its anticipated protections in place, is that society should encourage education and enlightenment. One way to accomplish that goal is to provide the means by which those who create things may be protected while they seek compensation for providing "copies" of their works for use by others.

For purposes of the ongoing discussion here, note that there is no such thing as an "international copyright." U.S. law and the treaties to which the U.S. is a party, will generally determine the protections afforded the work of a U.S. author in another country. Thus, the following discussion is based on U.S. Copyright Law.

COPYRIGHT "RIGHTS"

As previously noted, a copyright is something an author has in "an original work of authorship" that is "fixed in a tangible medium of expression."

The owner of a copyright enjoys the exclusive rights to:

- Reproduce the work
- Prepare derivative works of the work
- Distribute copies of the work by sale or other transfer of ownership, or by renting, leasing or lending the work
- Perform the work publicly
- Display the work publicly

These rights are not unlimited, and they are not "forever." Still, it is illegal for another party to violate someone's copyright rights. Indeed, infringements are deemed so serious, the law provides in some cases for "statutory damages," and in other cases, for criminal penalties, including fines and prison time.

Essentially, "statutory damages" allow for the harmed party not to have to "prove" the extent of his damages. Rather, the law provides a set amount (or more accurately, it provides for a range of amounts) for the injured party if the "statutory damages" option is open to him and he chooses to take it. These damage issues come into play when a copyright owner brings a civil action against another party for copyright infringement.

Criminal penalties for copyright infringement include possible fines (currently up to $250,000) and even prison sentences (currently for a first-time offense, up to five years). Why does the law provide for possible criminal actions against a copyright infringer? Well, the reason is simple, really. It is because the unauthorized copying of the work of another is *theft*. Depending on the value of what is stolen, that theft can amount to the equivalence of many, many dollars. In this way, the law provides criminal penalties in the same way it would if a thief entered your home and stole your heirloom silverware.

WHO OWNS THE COPYRIGHT?

Copyright protection comes into being from the time the artist/author puts his work into a "fixed form." A "fixed form" means that the work is in a form that may be perceptible directly or through the aid of a machine or device. For an author of a literary work, this means, when the work is put into writing that is readable in a print or electronic form. (Remember, we're not talking about protecting the *ideas* presented in a work, we're talking about the "form" those ideas take.)

Most often, the author—at least initially—is the "owner" of his own creations (and therefore the copyright owner) from the outset. There are, however, exceptions.

If, like me, you are the only party that contributed to the writing of your books (and they weren't created as "works for hire" as discussed below), you are the sole owner of the copyright to those works—unless or until you assign your rights to another party.

If a work is co-authored, both authors own rights in the work unless they have an agreement to the contrary.

EXCEPTIONS

As noted, there are exceptions to the "rule" that an author is the copyright owner. The first is when the circumstances involve an employer/employee relationship. If the employer assigns an employee the task of creating something, and that task is a part of the employee's employment, the employer is deemed the owner of the resulting work.

The second exception may arise if/when someone is hired to create a work for another party. Such works, called "works-for-hire" are discussed more fully, below.

The overall copyright principles are covered quite well in a U.S. Copyright Office publication that you will find available in the Copyright Office's Circular 1 (at https://www.copyright.gov/circs/circ01.pdf). Note its mention of certain things *not* deemed copyright protectable, including *titles* (although as we've discussed they may be protectable as trademarks, depending on whether they apply to more than one work), mere listings of ingredients or contents, and *ideas*.

Rights to a copyrighted work may be assigned and/or licensed to another party. This is discussed in more detail, later.

WORKS FOR HIRE

A work-for-hire is created when one party commissions another to create a work for them as a "work-for-hire" pursuant to a *written* agreement. Determining whether something is a "work for hire" can be complicated. The decision largely revolves around whether the party commissioning the work has control over the work being conducted, over the creator's schedule or means for accomplishing the task, and/or whether the party requesting the work provides benefits, or withholds taxes, for example, from the creator. If the person creating the work is an employee, no separate written agreement is needed. If that party is not an employee, a written agreement for the creation of the work is required. Further, *if* the parties expressly agree in a written document signed by the parties that the work is a work-for-hire, it will be deemed such *if* it was specially ordered or commissioned for use as:

- A contribution to a collective work
- A part of a motion picture or other audiovisual work
- A translation
- A supplementary work
- A compilation
- An instruction text
- A test
- As answer material for a test
- An atlas

Consider, for example, that you hire someone to create your book cover. Even if you specially commission someone to create it, the resulting work might not be deemed a "work-for-hire." (An exception, of course, would be if you are an employer and the creator is your employee who creates the work within the parameters of his employment.) Why? Because it's not likely you exercise the control over the creator that's required, and because the "cover" to a literary work would not likely fall into one of the categories noted above. Thus, if not a "work for hire," the artist who creates the cover will be the copyright owner of the resulting artwork (at least initially)—and you would be a mere licensee of the work.

Is there any way around this? Well, you cannot get around the law simply by your intention. You may, however, enter into a written agreement that provides that the resulting work will be deemed a work-for-hire. Even that, however, may not be sufficient. Thus, you should include *in that same document* that if for some reason the resulting work is not deemed to be a work-for-hire (by law), that the creator—by virtue of that written document—assigns his copyright rights in the work, to you.

Of course, if you are not the copyright owner of the resulting artwork that you use, you will want to make sure you know what your license to use that artwork authorizes you to do. (You will find more on licenses in Chapter 12.)

For more information on works for hire, see the Copyright Office's Circular 9 (at www.copyright.gov/circs/circ09.pdf).

GAINING COPYRIGHT

A work does not have to be published or registered to be copyright protected. Rather, copyright rights come into existence automatically when the work is "fixed in a tangible medium of expression." Even so, there are advantages to registering your work.

COPYRIGHT NOTICE: THE © SYMBOL

The copyright notice for a literary work consists of the © symbol (or the word "Copyright," or the abbreviation, "Copr"), the year of first publication, and the name of the copyright owner. Hence, my copyright statement for a work published in 2017, would read:

© 2017 Patricia Reding

The copyright notice should be in an obvious place. Indeed, most authors include a "copyright page" that sets out the information, along with such details as the ISBN number(s) assigned to the work, near the front of the book. For an unpublished work, I could use:

Unpublished work © 2017 Patricia Reding

Again, you do not have to use the copyright notice to have copyright rights in your work. However, the notice tells others that the work is protected by copyright. Also, it identifies the copyright owner, and it sets forth the year of first publication. This is important because, practically speaking, if someone infringes on a work that is not marked, the wrongdoer later may be able to claim lack of knowledge of the copyright as a defense to his act.

WHEN TO REGISTER – AS RELATES TO DAMAGES

There are no disadvantages—only potential advantages to be gained—with registering your copyright.

Ideally, you will register your work with the U.S. Copyright Office within three months after publication or prior to an infringement of the work. If you do so, statutory damages and attorney's fees may be available to you if you file an action for copyright infringement. Again, "statutory damages" is just a fancy way of saying that the law specifies a pre-determined amount (or up to a predetermined amount) for damages. In this context, "attorneys' fees" means that if you bring an action against someone else for their copyright infringement of your work, you may be able to get back from the wrongdoer, the cost of your attorney's fees related to your bringing the action.

If the situation does not give rise to statutory damages, an award of "actual damages" and profits is available to a copyright owner whose work is infringed.

Note that you may still register your work after the three-month period noted above, and the law will still provide you with added benefits, but the earlier registration is the goal. Thus, if you allow for someone who acts as an "agent" on your behalf to register your work for you, make sure the agreement provides that they will—and in fact that they do—make the filing within three months of publication.

MATERIALS NOT IDENTIFIED WITH THE © SYMBOL

Do you remember my saying earlier that if I had a nickel for every time someone told me he is flattered when someone reads his work—even if the reader's copy was pirated—that I could retire in luxury? The same holds true about this little fact: if I had a nickel for every time someone told me that they used something because they "found it on the Internet" and therefore, that it was in the public domain, available for their use, I could retire even sooner—and even wealthier!

Just because something isn't marked with the copyright symbol, doesn't mean it isn't copyright protected. Accordingly, it is always best and safest to make use only of those things you create for yourself or that you commission someone to create for you (with the appropriate agreement in place, of course!), or that you gain a license to any other works that you use. This holds true of written works, artwork used for your book covers, photos you use with your website materials (including for your blog posts), sound recordings that you add to your audio books, and so on.

LIFE OF A COPYRIGHT

Different rules apply to works created at different times. For many current authors today, the rule of interest is the rule applying to works originally created on or after January 1, 1978. For these works, copyright protection is automatic from the moment of creation. Thereafter, the protection is for a term enduring for the author's life—plus an additional 70 years after the author's death.

In the case of a joint work created on or after January 1, 1978, copyright protection applies for 70 years after the last surviving author's death.

For works-for-hire, anonymous, and pseudonymous works created on or after January 1, 1978 (unless the author's identity is revealed in the Copyright Office records), the copyright is for 95 years from the date of publication or 120 years from the date of creation, whichever is shorter.

After a copyright expires, the work is deemed to be in the public domain. At that point, a third person could "copy" the entire work and publish it without infringing the copyright.

AFTER DEATH

As you can see, when an author is deceased, the rights to her work continue for some time. Thus, copyright rights are valuable rights that may be "passed" after death via a person's last will and testament. (If the author should die without a will, the law will determine to whom the property will pass just as it would for other assets. For more information on this, see your legal counsel.)

ASSIGNING OR TRANSFERRING COPYRIGHT RIGHTS

A copyright owner may transfer all or part of his rights to another. To be valid, an *exclusive* transfer (by assignment or license) must be in writing and signed by the owner of the rights (or his duly authorized agent). A copyright owner may also allow someone to make use of some of his rights without assigning the underlying copyright or a portion of it, to the other party, via a *nonexclusive* license.

In practice, consider the rights a copyright owner enjoys. You will recall that one of those rights is the right to make copies of the work. When an author contracts with another party to print copies of his work, or to allow others to download e-copies of his work, those rights are part of the author's "exclusive" rights to reproduce the work.

To illustrate, when an author makes an e-book available through Amazon (for example), the author is entering into an agreement with Amazon. That agreement provides that Amazon may make copies of the work available to readers (to download them) in accordance with the terms of the author's agreement with Amazon. The agreement does not *assign* the author's copyright rights to reproduce the work, to Amazon. Rather, it is a *license* allowing Amazon to provide the copies. You can think of it this way: a "license" is essentially a promise not to sue the licensee, provided that the licensee's actions fall within the scope of what the license allows.

As for publishing companies, the terms of the agreement are key. Sometimes such agreements include an author's assignment of his copyright rights to the publisher, other times they merely license certain rights to the publisher. (So, once again, see legal counsel before you sign any document!)

Chapter 10
Copyright Registration

When you register your copyright, you are making a public record of the basic facts about your work and its ownership. Registration is not required for copyright protection. However, registration will provide the copyright owner with some added benefits.

THE ADVANTAGES OF REGISTRATION

The following will result from a copyright registration:

- It establishes a public record of the owner's claim, available for any third party to discover
- It allows the owner to bring an infringement action in federal court if the work originated in the U.S.
- If the registration was filed within five years after publication, it establishes prima facie evidence of the validity of the owner's claim (which means that he wouldn't later have to "prove" his ownership claim in an infringement action he might bring)

- If the registration is within three months after publication of the work, or prior to an infringement of the work, statutory damages and attorney's fees may be available to the owner in an infringement action (compared to only actual damages and loss of profits)
- Registration allows for an owner to register with the U.S. Customs Service to protect against unauthorized parties trying to import infringing copies of his work

These valuable rights are granted so as to encourage you to register your works. Thus, if you have not done so already, you might want to do that today. Legal counsel can assist you, but an attorney is not required to register a work. You may file for yourself, should you choose to do so.

FILING AN APPLICATION

If you are the author/creator of a work, you may file to register the work. Likewise, if you are the owner of a "work-for-hire" that someone else created for you under a "work-for-hire" arrangement.

To file an application, you will need to complete the application form. A copy of the print application form (called the TX form) for literary works is found at https://www.copyright.gov/forms/formtx.pdf. If you want to file online to register a literary work, you may do so using the Electronic Copyright Office (eCO) procedures. For information on online applications using eCO, see https://www.copyright.gov/registration/.

There is a fee for registering the copyright to your work. The fee will depend on the manner in which you file. Online filing is less expensive, goes faster, and allows you to track your application online.

When you register your copyright, you are required to provide certain copies of your work with the application. If you apply to register a literary work before it is published, you may provide as the required copies, electronic files for the work. If you register a literary work after it is published (whether with a paper application or by filing online), you will need to file two of the "best edition" copies of the work. Basically this means that if the book/work is available in hard cover, paperback, and as an e-copy, the "best edition" would be the hard cover. If the work is available only in paperback and e-versions, the "best available" would be the paperback version. Find out more about "best editions" at https://www.copyright.gov/circs/circ07b.pdf.

PUBLIC RECORD

The information filed with the U.S. Copyright Office is part of a public record, available for discovery by others. Thus, you may choose to use an address specifically for registration purposes that is separate and apart from your own home street address.

Chapter 11
Works with Various Copyright Protection Issues

When you prepare to file your work for copyright registration, you will want to consider what portions you may claim rights in/to.

THE TEXT

When you register your work for copyright, you are required to identify those portions of the work to which you claim rights. For example, for my literary works, I claimed protection only in the "text" portion of the books that I registered. The reason for this is that I did not create the artwork used for the covers and I am not the owner of those artworks. Thus, as I am not the original author/artist/creator of those portions of the books, and because those works were not assigned to me, I cannot claim copyright protection to those aspects of my books. The exception would be if I hired someone to create the work as a work-for-hire, in which case, I would still have to identify the actual creator of the work, in the copyright application, and I would then also have to include information as to how I came to be the copyright owner of that work. Likewise, if I became the owner by an assignment, I would have to identify the original creator, and then indicate how I came to be the copyright owner of the work.

THE COVER

When you hire a third party to create a cover for you, your book will include copies of that person's artwork. Thus, you will want to know that you have the right to, and that you may authorize others the ability to, make copies of your full work—which includes the cover. Accordingly, you will want to be sure that you know what your cover-creator is able to grant to you in terms of their rights of reproduction.

A cover creator may try to limit you to the number of book cover copies you can make that are covered by the license she grants you. She might not grant you the right to use the artwork on merchandise products, such as posters, T-shirts, or the like—so do not merely assume that you may create and market such goods. She may also provide you with a non-exclusive license to the use of the artwork that the cover encompasses. In such a case, you could find the same cover artwork used by other authors for their works. For these reasons, you want to be sure that you understand what is created for you when you have a book cover prepared, what rights you have to reproduce that work, and whether the artist may also authorize others to use the same artwork.

To complicate things, book cover designers often use artwork from other sources, such as Shutterstock. They get "licenses" to use photographs posted there, for particular purposes. Sometimes the rights granted to them are subject to limitations, which they then pass on to you through the (sub)license they extend to you.

For example, if my cover designer uses a photograph taken and owned by another party, my designer may only have rights to use that photograph in a certain manner, or to allow for only a certain number of copies of it be made. Thus, when my designer completes my cover, she would not be able to sub-license to me, greater rights than have been licensed to her. For this reason, I prefer to have my (fiction) covers designed by someone who I know took the photos herself, or who I know has gained exclusive rights to the use of the photographs that I select for my book covers. I also prefer if my cover creator is able to grant to me the *exclusive* rights to the *unlimited* use of a particular photo for my books and book promotional materials (including bookmarks, for example) so that I won't find the same artwork on other covers. Having said that, when I don't use works that meet such criteria, I want to be certain I know exactly what my cover creator does allow me to do with the final work.

ARTWORK FOR CHILDREN'S BOOKS

Do you create children's books? Do you have the artwork created for you as a work-for-hire? If so, be certain you have a written agreement with the artist. Such an agreement would effectively serve as the artist's affirmation that you are the copyright owner (even though the artist would still be identified as the artist/creator of those works in the copyright application). It would also be wise for you to have in the written "work-for-hire" agreement with the artist, a clause providing that the artist assigns his copyright rights in/to the artwork, to you, in the event it should be determined that the arrangement did not meet the "work-for-hire" requirements. That way, if the work-for-hire agreement is lacking in any way, or is deemed unenforceable for any reason, the artist would still already have assigned to you, all of his copyright rights in/to the artwork.

AUDIO BOOK RECORDINGS

As is the case with artwork created for your books, consider when entering the audio-book market, whether you want to be the sole copyright owner of the copyright in the *resulting recording*, or if the narrator (who is an "artist" whose work will be fixed in a tangible form of expression, namely, that *recording*) will own any copyright rights in that *audio* work. If you are the owner, you can do as you please in terms of making copies, and you may authorize others to do as you please. If the vocal artist is the owner, she could not publish copies without your permission (as they would be derivative works of your copyright protected work), but she could bar you from making copies of her artistic work without her permission. Of course, the work will only have value to the vocal artist if she allows you to publish the work (make copies or authorize another party to do so, and so forth). Thus, this really means that you and the vocal artist would have to negotiate over whether you will pay the artist an upfront fee for creating the recording, and/or what portion of the royalties each of you and the artist will earn with each copy of the work that is sold or otherwise distributed.

YOUR LOGOS

You may recall that I mentioned that logos—that is, design trademarks—that you use may also be copyright protectable. As these are original works of "authorship," set forth in "a tangible medium of expression," they constitute "artworks." As such, it is possible to claim copyright protection in a logo and even to register a logo for copyright. For more on these works, see U.S. Copyright Office, Circular 40 (at https://www.copyright.gov/circs/circ40.pdf).

If you use any design marks—logos—consider where the artwork for your logos came from. If you created them, you are the "author/artist" and the copyright owner. If someone else created them for you, you would be wise to take action to acquire an exclusive license to the use of the artwork for any and all purposes and for all time. Even better, you might acquire the copyright rights to the artwork by assignment. The reason is that you will want to know that you can use your logos whenever, wherever, and however, you want, and also, that you may use them as often as you like. (Of course, you can see how important it is, if you did not create the artwork for your logo yourself, that you know where it came from, as you would not want another party to claim that you have infringed their copyright to the artwork that your logo encompasses.)

Chapter 12
Copyright Assignments and Licenses

As previously noted, a copyright owner enjoys certain exclusive rights in/to a copyrighted work. He may assign or license those rights to others.

ASSIGNMENTS

If the owner wants to assign *all* of her copyright rights to another party, she may do so via an assignment of the copyright. As previously noted, such must be done in a written document. Once done, the author would have no remaining rights in the work. (Note that there is an "exception" if you will, under the Copyright Act, which *may* allow the creator or her heirs a "second chance" to exploit the work in certain situations where the value of the work may have increased significantly since the original transfer. For more information on this "quirk" and when it might apply, see your legal counsel.)

LICENSES TO OTHERS

A license is a vehicle a copyright owner may use to grant certain rights to another while maintaining ownership of the underlying copyright. As previously mentioned, it is basically a "promise not to sue" another party for actions he takes that would otherwise constitute copyright infringement.

Rights granted through a license may be exclusive or non-exclusive. Effectively, granting rights to another party means that the person to whom you grant rights, may take the actions you've allowed by virtue of the license, without fear of your bringing an infringement action against him.

Keep in mind the various different copyright rights that the owner enjoys. Thus, you could do all of the following—at the same time:

- License a publisher the right to reproduce and market your book
- License another party, the ability to create a screenplay of your work (which would be a "derivative" work)
- License a production company to create a movie of the work (which would be another derivation of your work)
- License a party to create an audio version of your book (which would be yet another derivation of your work)
- License a party to create toys or other merchandise products based on the characters in your book (and yes, this would be yet another derivative work)

In each case above, the rights you grant could be "exclusive" or "nonexclusive." Of course, you could also grant exclusive rights to a single party to do all of the above. (Keep in mind that exclusive licenses need to be in writing.)

LICENSES FROM OTHERS

Your book may include the work of others—such as the artwork used for your cover, the recorded audio for an audio book, or even the sound effects you use between "scenes" or as background music for your audio book. Unless you created those things yourself, someone else owns rights to them. Likewise, when you post blog articles in connection with which you include photographs, for instance, someone else owns the rights to those photographs (unless you took them yourself).

Since you offer your works commercially, you want to be sure that the licenses you have to use the works of others, allow for your *commercial* use of the works. For example, when I prepare blog articles, I sometimes use photographs from Pixabay (at https://pixabay.com). The reason I choose Pixabay pictures isn't because they have the best options available. Rather, it is because Pixabay provides that those who upload to Pixabay waive their copyright rights in their photos. Further, as a user of those photographs, I am free to adapt them and to use them for any purpose—even for a commercial purpose—without attributing the original author or source, or paying a fee. (Hopefully at this point you are finding the value to looking for the "terms" portions of websites such as Pixabay, as these issues may now have taken on a whole new level of importance to you.) (Oh, and mind you, the Pixabay terms could change at any time . . .)

LICENSES - EXCLUSIVE OR NONEXCLUSIVE

The natural reaction is to think that you would only ever want to grant "nonexclusive" rights to another so that you could grant additional nonexclusive rights to additional parties, thereby "hedging your bets." Be aware, however, that if a publisher is going to spend time and resources promoting your work for sale, that publisher is going to want to know that he will benefit from his efforts. Accordingly, he may not be willing to accept anything less than exclusive rights for making copies of your work, at least for some types of copies and/or in some territories.

Notwithstanding the above, you may be able to negotiate to grant someone certain exclusive rights that would be limited by a time period, or that would be dependent on that licensee's success. In other words, you might limit a publisher to the exclusive rights to publish for a period of say . . . three years. Alternatively, your contract might grant the exclusive rights for a limited period, but then also provide that if the publisher does not accomplish a certain level of sales, the license would terminate, or the assignment—if you granted the rights by an assignment to the publisher rather than by license—would revert back to you.

See your legal counsel to discuss these matters thoroughly before signing away any of your rights.

RESERVATIONS OF RIGHTS

It is imperative in this day of expanded avenues for generating revenue, when you enter into an agreement with another party that grants some rights to that party, that you carefully consider whether you want to reserve rights to grant copyright licenses to make derivative goods relating to visual aspects of your books. For example, if you write children's books, you may want to license a separate party to create toys modeled after your characters, or to print items ranging from notebooks to bed sheets, using your character images. (Of course, you can see the importance of your actually owning the copyrights to those images!) The typical "standard" or "boilerplate" contract that a publisher is likely to present to you at the start of your negotiations will not leave such "merchandising" rights to you. Thus, you may need to negotiate to retain these rights if you are interested in exploiting them through one or more other parties.

A NOTE ABOUT AUDIO BOOKS CREATED THROUGH ACX

ACX is an Amazon-related entity. It is a "marketplace" that brings together, authors, narrators, and others, to make the audio book creation easier. (Find out more at http://www.acx.com/help/about-acx/200484860.)

Audio Book Narration through ACX

If you are interested in having an audio book created through ACX, using an artist you connect with through ACX as the narrator, Amazon's online information provides that as *between you and ACX*, you will retain the rights (including the copyright rights) to the work. However, it will be important that you have in place, a contract between you and the *narrator* that provides for the same. Likewise, if you produce the work using an artist/narrator outside of the ACX system, you will want to be sure that the agreement you have with the artist sets out who will own the copyright in the finished *audio recording*. See the sample narration contract provided by ACX at www.acx.com/help/independent-contractor-agreements/200485560. Notice that it provides that the narrator, as an independent contractor, is providing the services as a "work-for-hire" to the extent the law allows, and that to the extent the law would not consider the work a "work-for-hire," that the narrator assigns all of his rights in the work—including the copyright rights in the finished audio book—to the party for whom the narrator is creating the work.

Distribution Rights

With ACX, your distribution rights to the finished audio book (as set forth on the site at http://www.acx.com/help/audiobook-license-and-distribution-agreement/201481900) will depend on whether you grant ACX exclusive distribution rights or non-exclusive distribution rights.

The current ACX contract (found online at the link noted above at the time of publication of this work) provides that if you grant ACX the exclusive license to use, reproduce, display, market, sell, and distribute, the audio book, throughout the territory (as defined in the agreement), those rights are for seven years from the date you accept the agreement. After that initial distribution period, the agreement will automatically renew for additional one-year terms unless either party provides notice of termination to the other at least 60 days in advance of the end of the initial distribution period (or of the then-current renewal period). During that time, you may not, nor may you permit any other party rights to, distribute, sell, or offer for sale (or even to give away copies of), the audio book anywhere else.

If you select to grant non-exclusive distribution rights, then you are granting ACX the non-exclusive license to use, reproduce, display, market, sell, and distribute, the audio book throughout the territory (as defined in the agreement) for the same seven-year initial distribution period. Again, the agreement will automatically renew for additional one-year terms unless either party provides notice to the other within the required period. The difference is that you may at the same time, and/or you may at the same time permit others to, distribute, sell, or offer for sale (or even give away copies of), the audio book, in the territory, during that period.

The standard ACX agreement grants ACX the right to use and distribute the cover art related to the audio book. Thus, you must be certain you have the right to grant that right to ACX.

The agreement sets out the royalty rates. As you may expect, they are higher if you grant ACX exclusive distribution rights. But remember that the royalty rate is not your *sole* concern. You might gain more in the long run if you are able to make the work available elsewhere—including through your own site, or as a free download, and so forth.

Artists/Narrators

An author (or a publisher, if the publisher holds the current rights to create audio books) may hire artists/narrators to create audio books through ACX. Loosely, the process means that the rights holder will post the title for creation, select a narrator, and decide on the payment method for the narration of the work. The rights holder may indicate that he will pay an hourly fee for the work, or he may choose to split the royalties with the narrator.

If you are the rights holder and you select to pay the narrator hourly, you may have more flexibility with what you may do with the work going forward. Of course, the up-front cost would be quite high. If instead, you choose to split the royalties from future sales with the artist, you will have to use ACX's exclusive distribution plan. If you think about it, this makes sense, because when you agree to split royalties, the narrator is risking her time and work in exchange for a share in the royalties. ACX, with its exclusive distribution procedures, will be able to account for all of the distributions made of the product and so, may split the royalties between the two parties when consumers purchase the product. Without exclusivity, ACX could not guarantee the narrator a share of the proceeds.

Of course, this also means that you cannot unilaterally decide to pull the product from the market at any time—even if ACX would otherwise agree to pull the product prior to the end of the then-current term of your ACX agreement. Rather, you would also need the narrator's consent before ACX would even consider allowing you to remove the product from the market. It also means that you might not be able to give away copies of the work, as you might benefit from the "giveaway" in some manner, while the artist/narrator might not.

One final note on audio books is that if you narrate your own, you will be considered both the producer and narrator through the ACX system. In such case, you would earn the full royalty that would otherwise be divided between those parties.

Chapter 13
Fair Use, Damages, and Criminal Penalties

A full discussion regarding possible damages in the event of a copyright infringement is beyond the scope of this work. However, in general, note that an infringer is liable for:

- The copyright owner's actual damages as well as additional profits the infringer realizes (damages and profits); or
- Statutory damages.

Before discussing damages for copyright infringement, let's take a look at situations in which you may be able to "copy" some portion of the work of another without a license to do so—and without that copying being deemed to be an "infringement."

THE "FAIR USE" DEFENSE

Do you remember that U.S. law recognizes copyright rights so as to encourage education and so that information will be made available to the marketplace? Well, the story does not end there. In fact, U.S. Copyright law also provides for an "exception" if you will, to the rights a copyright owner enjoys. The exception, traditionally called "fair use," was established so as to balance the rights of a copyright owner to society's interests to promote socially important activities. Those activities would include such things as news reporting, teaching, and commentary.

Fair use helps to promote free expression by allowing for the right to use certain information under some circumstances, even if that means using some portion of a copyright protected work. In essence, it is a "defense" to a claim of copyright infringement.

One *may* be able to use a portion of a copyright protected work (without a license from the copyright owner) without infringing on the copyright for such specific purposes as:

- Criticism
- Comment
- News Reporting
- Teaching
- Scholarship
- Research

Why do I say one *may* be able to do this? Quite simply because the use would have to be a "fair use."

To determine whether a use is "fair use," some of the following factors will be considered:

- The purpose of the use, including whether it was for a commercial purpose or for educational purposes
- The type or nature of the copyright protected work
- How much of the work was copied and how that portion compares to the "whole"
- The effect of the use on the potential market for the work

Fair use claims are determined on a case-by-case basis. In other words, it is not enough that you determine that your use of someone else's work or a portion of it is for an educational purpose and therefore, that it constitutes an acceptable "fair use." Likewise, you may not simply calculate that so long as you don't copy more than a certain percentage of an entire work, that your use of some portion of the work is a "fair use." Rather, the determination is highly sophisticated, taking the particular facts at issue into consideration. For these reasons, whenever you intend to include *any* portion of the work of another party in your work, you would do well to seek permission from the copyright owner to do so, in advance. For some basic information on "fair use" see material from the U.S. Copyright Office at https://www.copyright.gov/fair-use/more-info.html.

ACTUAL OR COMPENSATORY DAMAGES

In an infringement action, the copyright owner may be able to recover "actual"—also called "compensatory"—damages. Essentially, this is the amount of any demonstrable loss the owner suffered as a consequence of the infringer's activity. Losses can include lost sales, lost licensing revenue, and other financial losses directly attributed to the infringement. The owner may also recover the infringer's "profits."

The infringer is required to prove his or her deductible expenses and the elements of profit that are attributable to factors other than the copyrighted work.

STATUTORY DAMAGES

Sometimes the owner may find it difficult to prove actual damages and lost profits. Thus, in certain circumstances, the copyright owner may elect, in lieu of actual damages and profits, an award of statuary damages.

Statutory damages are amounts set by law. When the owner cannot prove that the infringement was either innocent or willful, statutory damages may range from $750 to $30,000 per infringement (that is, per work), depending on the circumstances and as the court considers "just." If it is determined that the infringement was innocent, the damages could be reduced to as little as $200 (per infringed work), whereas if willful, the statutory damages could be increased up to $150,000 (per infringed work). Basically, the amount depends on the seriousness of the situation and the infringer, itself. As statutory damages may be available to a copyright owner who registers his work within three months of its publication or before actual infringement, it is important to see to the filing of your works as quickly as possible following their publication.

CRIMINAL PENALTIES

The act of a copyright infringement may be deemed a criminal act if the infringer knew she was committing a crime. In the event it is determined that a crime has been committed, the offender may be fined up to $250,000, and even imprisoned for up to five years, for a first offense. (These figures are current as of the time of publication of this work.) Indeed, copyright infringement is no joke!

Chapter 14
The Digital Millennium Copyright Act (DMCA)

The Digital Millennium Copyright Act (the "DMCA"), signed into law in 1998, came about following the quick expansion of the use of the Internet by the general populace. It provides for protections against online copyright infringement for Internet service providers (ISPs), search engines, website hosts, or other site-managers (collectively referred to going forward as ISPs), and for copyright owners.

TAKE DOWN

The DMCA gives a copyright owner (whether or not the work is copyright registered) a way to request removal of her copyright protected material that another party posts online. Essentially, the law is intended to get ISPs and copyright owners to work together to identify and to address online copyright infringements. The law "protects" the ISP from liability for copyright infringement by its users, provided that the ISP meets certain conditions.

The theory behind the protection that the DMCA offers an ISP is that an ISP may not be aware of what its customers are posting online. Thus, the DMCA allows for an ISP to designate an agent to receive notices of claimed copyright infringements. The ISP is to provide, on its website, contact information for its DMCA agent. The ISP then provides the same information to the U.S. Copyright Office. In turn, the U.S. Copyright Office keeps a directory of designated ISP agents identified by various ISPs. Wronged parties may contact an ISP agent of the online infringement of their work when found on a site provided by that ISP.

When a copyright owner learns of a violation of his copyright that is set forth on a website, he can send a notice of the infringement, to the ISP. In practice, to be protected against a claim of copyright infringement, the ISP must:

- Not have actual or constructive knowledge of the infringing behavior
- Not experience financial benefit from the infringement
- When given proper notice that infringing materials have been posted, respond quickly to remove, or to disable access to, the materials that the owner claims are infringing

The ISP will contact its customer, giving that party the opportunity to voluntarily comply with the DMCA notice—that is, to remove the infringing material. If the party does not comply, the ISP must do so if the ISP wants to avoid being held responsible for the copyright infringement.

When You Need Protection

In practice, if I find that another party has "copied" my work and has posted it on that party's blog, or that the party copied my book and is allowing for others to download pirated copies of it from its website, I can notify the ISP agent for the blog or site, of that infringement. Before doing so, I want to know that I am the rightful copyright owner, and that the materials posted do not constitute "fair use."

To file a complaint, I would:

- Locate the correct person and then write that person, identifying the infringing work
- Provide the ISP agent with the means to contact me
- Note that I have a good faith belief that the use of the material I am informing them of is not authorized by me (the copyright owner), my agent, or the law
- Include a statement that the information I am providing is accurate and that under penalty of perjury, I am authorized to make the request

Locating the correct person can be difficult. The first step would be to identify the domain name registrar or the website hosting company for the site where the material is found. Often you can find this information on the "whois" page for the domain name used for the site. One option is to go to https://whois.icann.org/en, and enter the domain name address to get information on the registrant. What you are looking for is the name of the hosting ISP. Another option is to use the services of parties that offer DNS lookup options (often for a fee). These services are sometimes able to provide better information.

The DMCA agent for an ISP is often found on the party's website, sometimes clearly identified as such. Other times it may be found in the "legal" or other "terms" provided on the site.

Many ISPs provide a DMCA form on their site. Often using the form to file is your best option, as with it, you will be sure to include the information required. Also, you may get a quicker response using the ISPs own form. If no form is provided, identify whether the ISP will receive requests by email, or only in some other manner.

If I do all of these things and the ISP promptly removes the offending materials, the ISP will not be held liable for copyright infringement (provided it hadn't engaged in other wrongdoing relating to the infringement). If I do not get satisfaction in this manner, my options would include filing suit for copyright infringement.

When You are the Accused Wrongdoer

If you turn the tables, you can see that it may be that you are making use of materials on your website—perhaps something you consider to be a "fair use" or a parody—that you think are not infringing the copyright rights of another. If your ISP receives a notice claiming that your use is an infringing use, your ISP is not likely to engage in much of an investigation. Rather, your ISP may simply remove the materials or block your site—so as to avoid being held liable for copyright infringement, itself. (Thus, you can see the importance of, for example, only using photographs on your website or blog that you know you created, or that you can prove you have the right to use.)

If your ISP removes items from your site or blocks your site following receipt of a DMCA claim, you may provide a "counter-notice" to your ISP. Thereafter, your ISP may decide to restore access to the material. From that point—as I'm sure you can imagine—things get complicated. To get resolution, you as the copyright owner, may need to file an actual copyright infringement action. Likewise, if you are the party using the materials, you may need to prepare yourself to respond to a copyright infringement action brought against you.

Non-U.S. Sites

Notwithstanding the above, it is often the case that sites pirating materials are located outside of the U.S. and therefore, that they are outside the reach of U.S. law enforcement. In those circumstances, it is likely that a DMCA request (or demand, if you will), will be (sadly) ignored. At such times, you would be wise to contact your legal counsel.

Chapter 15
Publishing Contracts

When it comes to publishing contracts, remember that while your agent may be doing the negotiating with a publisher on your behalf (at least initially—before you get your legal counsel involved), it is important that you understand the issues. Those of most concern to you will likely concentrate on what trademark and/or copyright rights—that is, what intellectual property rights—you are licensing or assigning and what you will get in exchange for them.

Will the copyright license that you grant pertain only to reproduction rights? Film rights? Audio rights? Merchandising rights? Foreign translations? Or are you assigning those rights? If by license, for what period will those rights be licensed? For a specified limited time? For the life of your copyright? If by an assignment, are there conditions under which the underlying rights would revert back to you? What forms of media will be covered? Hard cover books only? Paperback only? E-books? Will the agreement cover other forms of merchandise? Posters? Stuffed animals? In what territories may the publisher exploit the rights? Only in the U.S.? Worldwide? The decisions you make regarding such agreements could have very long-term consequences.

With these agreements, often an author's first concern is over how many printed copies will be provided to him, or what photo of him the publisher will use in its promotional materials. In fact, however, there are many potential issues to consider when it comes to your granting assignments and/or licenses of your work. The issues are vast—and they are complicated. Indeed, an in-depth discussion of them is beyond the scope of this handbook. However, it will help you to know something about these issues as you prepare to discuss them with your legal counsel.

Keep in mind that if a publisher is interested in publishing your work because the publisher believes that the work has promise, it is expected that you will have questions, and that you will want to negotiate particular terms. Likely, the opportunity to get things that you want will never be greater.

DUE DATES

Of course, if the work at issue is not yet created at the time you sign an agreement, you will want to spell out when you are due to provide your manuscript and in what format you will provide it.

EDITORIAL SERVICES

Your agreement should cover what editorial services the publisher will provide to you. But what if you find errors after the publisher's editor has completed her work? And what if they are errors that may, in the long run, reflect poorly on you and your work? Would the agreement require that you accept the editor's recommended changes?

Also, negotiate whether the publisher may alter your work and, if necessary, what will happen if the publisher (through editing) alters your story or its characters in a manner that you find objectionable.

Finally, you might clarify that all copyright rights to any editing changes or additions belong solely to you.

TERRITORY

Likely you won't want to grant your publisher worldwide rights if your publisher only offers items published in the English language. In addition, you probably won't want to grant to your publisher, movie rights, or audio book rights—unless your publisher will also make use of those rights. In other words, if the publisher is not going to "exploit" those rights so as to generate revenue for itself—and for you—then you may be better served if you do not tie up those rights with that party. On the other hand, you might "share" such rights, thereby encouraging the publisher to make the most of your work, while still retaining the ability to earn more if your work results in a significant following.

COVER DESIGN

Think about what input you would like to have in the cover design for your work. You may want to include that you have the right to approve and/or to reject proposed cover art for your work. Also, take note of whether you will have the right to make use of the same cover following the termination of your agreement for any reason. It may be the case that the publisher only has a license to reproduce the cover from the artist that designed/created the cover and therefore, that owns the copyright to that work. In such event, the publisher might not have any rights in the cover artwork to assign to you upon termination of the agreement.

ADVANCE PAYMENTS

If payment is to be made as an "advance," you may minimize the likelihood of misunderstanding about when that payment will be made, by setting out a date you control, such as "within ten days of *the author's* execution" of the agreement.

MEDIA AND ROYALTIES

If the contract is to cover a variety of forms of media, be certain it indicates the royalties applicable to each. For example, the royalty on an e-book could differ from the royalty for a paperback copy and/or from the royalty assigned to a hard cover copy. Also, whenever possible, have the royalties defined in a manner that will allow for you to more easily calculate them.

You might request a change in royalty in the event the work meets a certain number of sales, or is categorized as a "best seller," or if it becomes an award winner of some type.

After spelling out carefully what rights of publication you are granting to the publisher, consider having the agreement specifically provide that you retain any rights not granted to the publisher.

CALCULATION OF AND ACCOUNTING FOR ROYALTIES

Give some consideration to the information you will want about how and when royalties will be earned and calculated, when they will be paid, and whether portions of your royalties will be reserved in the event copies are returned and/or in the event a claim is made against you and/or the publisher relating to the work (such as a copyright infringement claim, or a defamation claim, for example).

COPYRIGHT REGISTRATION

If the publisher's duties will include filing for copyright registration, the agreement should require the publisher do so within 90 days of the date of publication. If it provides that you will register the copyright—or is silent on the issue—be sure that you see to the matter.

PUBLICATION

Consider the duties of the publisher, such as when the book is to go public. What happens if the publisher does not meet the requirements? You might want to provide that if the publisher does not accomplish a certain deed by a specified date, that you can terminate the contract and retain any advance previously paid to you.

LIKENESS

Review terms regarding whether, and if so, how, the publisher may use your name and likeness.

REVIEWS

Will your publisher offer copies for reviews? How many? Over what period of time? May the reviewers re-sell those copies or may the publisher only provide them to parties who agree to destroy them?

ADVERTISING AND PROMOTION

A publishing agreement will likely cover what efforts the publisher will make to advertise and to promote your work. How and where will the work be advertised? Will the publisher send you on a book promotional tour? If so, where will they send you and for how long? At whose expense will you go on tour and what accommodations can you expect? Will you be able to perform as required? These are all issues for your consideration.

MERCHANDISING RIGHTS

You may want to retain the rights to license your name or other trademarks that you use in connection with your books—such as series titles, *character names and images*, and the like. Be prepared to negotiate to retain merchandising rights if you are interested in doing so.

FUTURE RESTRICTIONS

Once the agreement is in place, will you be able to write competing works on topics similar to those covered in the work at issue? Will you be required to offer your next work to this same publisher before you can "shop it out" to others?

In the event you cancel the agreement according to its terms, can you enter into a new arrangement with a new publisher right away? Can you immediately self-publish the same or other works? Or will you be required to wait a period of time before doing so? Also, again, consider whether you'll be able to make use of the same cover art if you re-publish on your own after termination of the agreement.

REVERSION OF RIGHTS

Your agreement might include terms relating to the reversion of rights to you when the agreement terminates. You might also add that if/when the royalties do not meet a certain level for one or more years, that the rights to publish the work will revert back to you.

AUTHOR REPRESENTATIONS

Expect that the publisher will want you to represent, with respect to your work, that:

- It is your own work only
- No other party has any valid copyright claim to the work or any portion of it
- No other party has any valid trademark claim relating to the work or any portion of it or of any features of it
- The work does not defame another
- The work does not infringe on the privacy rights of another

- That you have not previously granted rights to another party that you purport to grant in the agreement at hand

The publisher may propose retaining some portion of earned royalties for use in the event claims are brought in connection with the work with respect to any of these issues.

INSURANCE

What if someone brings a claim against your work? Suppose, for example, that someone claims that your work infringed on her copyright. Consider whether you will carry insurance against such a possibility, or whether your publisher will do so and, if the publisher will carry the insurance, whether it will cover you as well as the publisher.

Pay attention to terms regarding when and how the publisher may settle claims such as copyright infringement or defamation claims that third parties may bring. What if your publisher chooses not to defend against a claim because of the expense the publisher would experience to do so—even though you maintain your innocence? If the publisher "settles," how will this affect your royalties? Your reputation?

LOOSE LANGUAGE

Watch for phrases such as “including, but not limited to,” or “usual and customary,” or “similar media, which may be created hereafter.” Consider for example, that current technology allows for print, audio, and e-books. But what if a new technology is introduced that revolutionizes any of these forms in such a manner that your rights would be compromised based on a “similar media” clause in an old agreement? For example, e-books are a relatively new option. Would a “similar media” clause back in the day of print-only books have allowed for e-copies?

Of course, some legal phrasing in a final agreement may not be entirely unavoidable. For example, it may be necessary to provide in the end, that the publisher will use its “best efforts” in promoting and selling your work. Even so, in general, the more specifically something is spelled out, the better. Having said that, once you start identifying particulars, keep in mind that a later reading of the document may not cover a particular scenario because it was *not* spelled out in the agreement.

LEGAL COUNSEL

Once again: if you never before enlisted the services of legal counsel, the time for a contract review would *not* be the time to short-change yourself!

Chapter 16
A Brief Review of Some Miscellaneous Issues

In addition to trademark and copyright issues, an author may at times, face additional legal issues.

DEFAMATION

An author needs to use care in what he says about others. To defame someone is to make a false statement about them in print (libel) or when speaking (slander). The laws of various states will determine the damages a defamed party may seek.

RIGHTS OF PRIVACY

The laws of the various states also recognize the rights of individuals to "privacy." These rights may differ from state to state, and the remedies afforded the wronged party may also differ. The rights to privacy include the right to one's own name and likeness, and to the public disclosure of certain facts.

USE OF ONE'S LIKENESS

If you are ever interested in using the name or likeness of another, or to publish something about another, you would be wise to seek legal counsel to discuss such issues before you go to print. Likewise, if you believe yourself to have been defamed, or find your name and/or likeness has been used without your permission, or you find your own privacy to have been violated, contact your legal counsel.

ISBN IDENTIFIERS

In addition to issues relating to trademarks and copyrights, authors frequently have questions about ISBNs. Accordingly, I am adding this short discussion for your consideration. I do so, in part, because these issues could affect what you can do with your work.

What is an ISBN and What Purpose Does One Serve?

An ISBN is an International Standard Book Number. It is used to identify a specific book for booksellers, libraries, distributors, and others. ISBN numbers historically, were 10 digits in length, but for about a decade now, have consisted of 13 digits.

In the U.S., all ISBN numbers are assigned through Bowker (at http://www.bowker.com). That is, Bowker is the agency authorized by U.S. Law to assign ISBNs for works published in the U.S. (If you receive an ISBN number from another party, that party actually purchased the ISBN through Bowker.)

Purchasing ISBNs

You may purchase, for each definitive different work, a separate ISBN. Because the ISBN number identifies the specific details for the item, such as the *format* of the book, as well as other important information, each different format of the same "work," receives its own ISBN. In other words, if I have a single work that I will publish in hard cover, paperback, EPUB, and audio book forms, I would assign to each of those forms, a separate ISBN. Thus, one should not attempt to use an ISBN for a paperback copy in connection with the EPUB version of the same work.

What is an ASIN?

To complicate matters, some entities allow for you to publish an e-book through them, without assigning a different ISBN to the book. Most notable is Amazon, which assigns each e-book its own ASIN—a book identifier used for *Amazon's* system. Since Amazon is the only e-book distributor that uses the MOBI form, the ASIN that Amazon assigns would only apply to the MOBI form of your e-book available through Amazon. An Amazon ASIN will be assigned to your e-book even if you have assigned an ISBN to that MOBI form e-book.

ISBNs Provided by Others

Amazon will allow you to publish your paperback through CreateSpace. If you do so, you may choose whether you will:

- Assign an ISBN that you purchased to the work
- Purchase an ISBN through Amazon that will allow you to use your own publisher's imprint and distribute the work anywhere you like
- Allow CreateSpace to assign a "free" ISBN to the work for you (in which case, you may not use your own publisher's imprint, and you may not distribute the work through other parties)

As you see, if you use the "free" option, you may *not* use your own publisher's imprint for the work and you may *not* publish that same work through other services—such as through IngramSpark. In other words, you have in some manner, restricted what you can do with that work to which that ISBN is assigned. For this reason, you might consider purchasing your own ISBN from the outset. (As one who originally did not for some of my first works, I can tell you that this could save you a great deal of headache down the road.)

Illustrate This, Please!

To illustrate how this works, I will discuss how I handled the ISBN and ASIN number issues for this book. First, I signed up for an account with Bowker. Then, I waited. You see, I knew that, occasionally, Bowker puts ISBNs "on sale." This is important, because the cost for a *single* ISBN, at normal rates, is $125 (at the time of this publication). This means that if I had a hardcover, a paperback, and an EPUB version for a single work, it would cost me a total of $375 to get ISBNs for them all. If I then added an audio version, I'd be up to $500. By contrast, I purchased ten (or more) ISBNs for a much lower per-ISBN price, simply by waiting for a sale.

When you purchase one or more ISBNs from Bowker, you will access the information for those ISBN(s) at https://www.myidentifiers.com. Through that link, you will "assign" one ISBN to each format for your work. As you assign the numbers, you will be required to provide information about the format of the book, its length, and so forth.

For this work (*Ignorance is Not Bliss*), I have paperback and e-book forms available. The e-book forms include an EPUB version, and a MOBI version. I have assigned one ISBN for the paperback version and one for the EPUB version. I did not assign a separate ISBN for the MOBI version—available only through Amazon—because it will be assigned its own ASIN through Amazon and wouldn't be available elsewhere anyway. Of course, I could assign an ISBN to the MOBI version of the book. I simply chose not to, so as to save some money. Mind you, it is not my "recommendation" that you do the same. I am merely sharing what I decided to do.

Purchasing Your Own ISBNs

Some time ago I published a couple of books in print and e-book form only, through CreateSpace. For my paperback books, I elected to use "free" ISBNs that CreateSpace assigned.

What this meant was that I could not make those same paperback books available through other parties—such as IngramSpark—using the same ISBNs. Many authors choose the free CreateSpace option, as I did, because Amazon still allows the author to opt for "extended distribution." Therefore, these works are supposed to be available to other parties, such as bookstores, schools, and libraries.

In actual practice, many people suggest that book distributors and bookstores often will not purchase from Amazon. Rather, they will only purchase through IngramSpark (related to Lighting Source). Thus, I've concluded that if I can't get bookstores and similar buyers to purchase from Amazon/CreateSpace anyway, then it really doesn't matter if I sign up for CreateSpace's extended distribution program. Accordingly, for those earlier works that I had published with CreateSpace's free ISBNs, I removed the books from CreateSpace, prepared a "new" copy of each to which I assigned my own ISBN number, and then re-loaded the works to CreateSpace. I then elected *not* to use Amazon's extended distribution program. At the same time, I also made the same books with the same ISBNs available through IngramSpark. In this way, a single ISBN for the same paperback book was all I needed to offer it through both CreateSpace and IngramSpark.

As mentioned, I also assigned an ISBN to the EPUB versions of my books. I then had the option of making the EPUB versions available through IngramSpark to various distributors, or I could choose to go directly to each distributor, or I could use another distributor service, such as Draft2Digital at https://www.draft2digital.com. By assigning an ISBN to the

EPUB version, I can make that same EPUB item available through various sources with a single ISBN.

Finally, as mentioned, I did not assign an ISBN to the MOBI version, which is only available on Amazon—although I certainly may have chosen to do so.

FINAL THOUGHTS

As noted at the outset, this work was not intended to be a definitive resource for authors for all things legal. Rather, it was intended to serve as a resource for answering general questions about your intellectual property rights—and in some cases, your responsibilities. Of course, as I am not your legal counsel, I cannot speak to the specific issues you face. However, I hope that the information in this primer will serve you as you choose future titles, register your copyrights, and more. Certainly, the more you understand about these issues, the more you can participate in discussions with your legal counsel when you do engage the services of an attorney.

I wish you great success with your endeavors!

ADDITIONAL RESOURCES

Trademarks

Trademark Basics: https://www.uspto.gov/trademarks-getting-started/trademark-basics

Basic Facts Booklet:
https://www.uspto.gov/sites/default/files/documents/BasicFacts.pdf

Online (TESS) Trademark Search:
https://www.uspto.gov/trademarks-application-process/search-trademark-database

Online Trademark Application:
https://www.uspto.gov/trademarks-application-process/filing-online

Trademark Electronic Application System (TEAS) Basics:
https://www.uspto.gov/learning-and-resources/trademark-faqs

Trademark Assistance Center:
https://www.uspto.gov/learning-and-resources/support-centers/trademark-assistance-center

Maintaining Your Registration: https://www.uspto.gov/trademarks-maintaining-trademark-registration/keeping-your-registration-alive

Transferring Trademark Ownership: https://www.uspto.gov/trademark/trademark-assignments-change-search-ownership

Been Sued?: https://www.uspto.gov/trademark/been-sued-or-received-cease-and-desist-letter-answers-common-questions-about-trademark

Trademark Tuesday Video Conferences: https://www.uspto.gov/about-us/uspto-locations/silicon-valley-ca/trademark-tuesday-13

Trademark Information Network Videos: https://www.uspto.gov/trademarks-getting-started/process-overview/trademark-information-network

Copyrights

Copyright Basics: https://www.copyright.gov/circs/circ01.pdf

Works Made for Hire: https://www.copyright.gov/circs/circ09.pdf

Copyright Notice: https://www.copyright.gov/circs/circ03.pdf

Copyright Circulars: https://www.copyright.gov/circs/

Duration: https://www.copyright.gov/circs/circ15a.pdf

Frequently Asked Questions:
https://www.copyright.gov/help/faq/

U.S. Customs Service: www.cbp.gov

Copyright Search: http://cocatalog.loc.gov/cgi-bin/Pwebrecon.cgi?DB=local&PAGE=First

Best Editions: https://www.copyright.gov/circs/circ07b.pdf

History/Education: https://www.copyright.gov/history/

DMCA Information: https://www.copyright.gov/dmca-directory/

Fair Use: https://www.copyright.gov/fair-use/more-info.html

Fair Use Decisions: https://www.copyright.gov/fair-use/

Electronic Copyright Office:
https://eco.copyright.gov/eService_enu/start.swe?SWECmd=Start&SWEHo=eco.copyright.gov

ISBNs

Bowker at http://www.isbn.org/faqs_general_questions

Audible Audio Books

ACX (an Amazon company) at http://www.acx.com/help/authors/200484540?utm_medium=author&utm_campaign=hiwtable

Audible Q&A: http://audible-acx.custhelp.com/app/browse/c/3556,3560

ABOUT THE AUTHOR

Multi-award winning author Patricia Reding leads a double life. By day, she practices law. By night, she reads, reviews a wide variety of works, and writes. She lives on an island on the Mississippi with her husband and youngest daughter (her son and oldest daughter having already flown the nest), and Flynn Rider (an English Cream Golden Retriever). From there she seeks to create a world in which she can be in two places at once.

Patricia has practiced intellectual property law for . . . decades. She assists clients with protecting their trademarks and copyrighted materials. With her 2017 publication of *Ignorance is Not Bliss: A Primer for Authors – Protect Your Work and Yourself*, she offers authors general information, prompting them to be more aware of potential issues and encouraging them to ask the right questions so as to better protect their works and themselves.

For more information visit the author on her website at www.PatriciaReding.com. You will also find her on:

Facebook:
https://www.facebook.com/PatriciaRedingAuthor

Goodreads:
https://www.goodreads.com/author/show/6983212.Patricia_Reding

Booklikes:
http://patriciareding.booklikes.com

Bublish:
https://www.bublish.com/author/view/6479

Google+:
https://plus.google.com/+PatriciaReding

Instagram:
http://www.instagram.com/patriciareding

Twitter:
http://www.instagram.com/PatriciaReding7

A NOTE FROM THE AUTHOR

I thank you for your kind attention to *Ignorance is Not Bliss: A Primer for Authors – Protect Your Work and Yourself.* I hope you found the materials helpful. I would be delighted if you would take a minute to leave a review on your favorite book vendor's site, your blog, or elsewhere. Also, please share information about this resource with your author friends who may benefit from it. Thank you!

Made in the USA
Columbia, SC
07 August 2021